FAR OUT DINKY DI

How Australia Was Won

Rod Kluzki

Far Out

Dinky Di

Winnty Publishing

ISBN: 978-0-9876214-4-3

Copyright © 2016 Rado Folwarczny

All rights reserved. No part of this book may be reproduced in any form by any means without the express written permission of the author. While every effort is made to ensure the accuracy of information at the time of publication, changes in circumstances may occur. The publisher accepts no liability or responsibility to any person or organisation as a consequence of any reliance upon the information contained in this book. Characters portrayed in this book are based on real people but some of their names were changed.

This book was written by a human.

Contents

Introduction — 13

I. Turning Upside Down — 14

1. Cook's Syndrome: Australia Is More — 15
2. Underdogs to Explorers — 16
3. Everybody Can: No Pain No gain — 20
4. Crash Course in Australian Basic Education — 24
5. Driving Thingybob and the Holy Licence — 26
6. Indigenous Versus Conventional: Take I — 30
7. The Case Nullius and Terra Mabo — 31
8. Hatch, Hatch, Hatchback — 36
9. Slowly, Slowly Catchee Possum — 39
10. Pavlova — 43
11. Off Ya Go — 45

II. Perth to Broome — 49

12. At the Bottom of the Sea: Pinnacles — 49
13. Spider from Nerren Nerren — 52
14. Pouring Buckets: Monsoon Rain — 55
15. From Sea to Mountains — 57

16 Iron Prince of Pilbara: Tom Price	61
17 The Nanny	64
18 Walking On Ore: Karijini National Park	68
19 Salt, Tibet And the Prophecy of Port Hedland	74
20 Great Sandy Desert	76
21 Indigenous Versus Conventional: Take II	79
22 Tourist Broome	83

III. Broome to Darwin — 87

23 "That Funny Hotel": From Fitzroy to Halls	87
24 Vanishing Tourists Business	92
25 United We Fall	94
26 Of Crocodiles and Men: Take I	97
27 Castration as a Job: Kununurra	101
28 Sea in the Desert: Lake Argyle	106
29 Customs and Public Holidays: NT Border	111
30 Spa Time: Katherine is Hot, Douglas is Cool	114
31 Darwin in a Nutshell	119

IV. Darwin to Alice Springs — 121

32 Where You Only Swim in a Pool: Kakadu	121
33 Of Crocodiles and Men: Take II	125
34 Flying in the Bush: Mataranka	127
35 Alice in Wander Land	131

36	Road to Nowhere: West MacDonnell Ranges	135
37	On a Bike Through Desert	139

V. New Look At the Red Centre   142

38	Where Things Howl: Uluru aka Ayers Rock	142
39	Sexy Walls: Kata Tjuta and Kings Canyon	149
40	Coroner on Vacation	151
41	Busting Dingo	152
42	Where Mad Max Drove: Breakaways	154

VI. White Bloke Down a Pit   156

43	Opal Land: the Ingenuity of Coober Pedy	156
44	Indigenous Versus Conventional: Take III	162
45	Welcome and Piss Off: Find and Not to Lose	164
46	Firecracker Town: Woomera	170

VII. Port Augusta to Melbourne   172

47	Tough Luck Mountains: Flinders Ranges	172
48	Adelaide in a Nutshell	177
49	Fifty Thousand Years Ago: Naracoorte	178
50	All Seasons in One Day: Grampians	181
51	What the Guides Won't Say: Peaks of Grampians	183
52	Clay and Whales: Great Ocean Road	188
53	Melbourne in a Nutshell	190

54 Eureka: How Much Does a Dream Cost	192
55 Uncle Chopper And Papa Rog	197

VIII. Melbourne to Sydney — 203

56 Mister Ricketts' Beautiful Soul	203
57 North Over the Hill Country	205
58 Why Mount Kosciuszko	206
59 Canberra in a Nutshell	211
60 Mountains Upside Down	212

IX. Big Smoke — 217

61 Where Freedom Begins: Hill End	217
62 It's Panning Out	221
63 In Which Otto Won his Lotto	223
64 Epilogue	226
GLOSSARY	230
Map	234
Noteworthy Mountains and Peaks	235
Route and Refuelling	236
Travel Budget Hints	241
Not to forget	242
Bibliography	244
Index	245

FAR OUT

mild expletive, a moderate exclamation, pronounced slowly with emphasis on the first letter 'F'. It has many meanings - from awesome or cool to extraordinary, it is an expression of disbelief, agreement, delight or surprise, it can describe something that is very hard to understand, strange, mysterious or even crazy, something that is extremely unconventional, unusual or eccentric. It can suggest that something is outlandish, but also excellent, wonderful, radical, or generally regarded as serious or intense it can also express admiration for something that is either interesting or bizarre. It is used when you have an urge to say 'fuck!' but there are small children around.

DINKY DI

really, truly, for real, true, genuine, honest. Australian slang.

Introduction

Shortly before the beginning of the third millennium, a runaway horse had set out on a quest to swim from the South Australian coast down to Antarctica. An all-volunteer rescue team struggled for hours to get the hapless animal out of the water, and before they could, it nearly drowned.

Far out! From that moment on, I longed for a glimpse of a country where horses are lined up on the seashore, ready to charge into the breaking waves without warning, so that ever larger formations of rescuers can follow in their wake to save them. It is almost impossible to judge the world by the daily news.

I stuffed my rucksack with a few wrinkled T-shirts, two pairs of well-worn hiking boots, threw in a reasonably large chunk of courage, a few slices of self-denial, a soon-to-expire sachet of pulverised common sense, salted with a lot of naive expectations, and on a very limited budget I went to check it out. Since Australians were still unsure whether or not their country had been discovered, I was here to answer that question once and for all.

Every place has a soul and every stone has a story to tell. Travel is the ultimate eye-opener. Forget for a moment the politically correct, carefully presented, neatly combed Australia that is sold around the world, and dive instead into the lesser-known, uncensored, three-dimensional version. The first dimension is space—you have to be physically somewhere to experience it first hand, and ideally spend some time there. The second dimension is the past—you need to understand what things were like before you got there in order to make an educated guess as to what they are likely to be in the future. But the third and most important dimension is people. If you can get away from the big cities with their poisonous souls and dare to take the roads less travelled, you'll meet locals who will tell you more than all the travel guides put together—the sort of thing you won't find in any official news portal. This is especially true for Australia. Bon voyage!

I. Turning Upside Down

I am landing in Sydney and Australia is lying at my feet.

The TV crews are getting their gear ready, the brass bands and sexy cheerleaders are in full swing, my name is in the headlines and the red carpet is ready to roll. The colourful glitter has filled the sky and turned it into a magnificent spectacle of joyous celebration.

Hardly off the plane, I am swallowed by a crowd of greedy journalists. Their microphones and cameras are kissing my head. The whole country has come to a standstill.

I am the ONE they have all been waiting for.

Then the music stops.

I wake up in a cheap backpackers on the outskirts of a big city with beads of sweat running down my forehead. It's my first night in Australia.

But I'm getting ahead of myself. First things first.

1
Cook's Syndrome: Australia Is More

At the corner of Park and College Streets, in more or less the middle of a green city patch called Hyde Park, in the continent's largest city of Sydney, there is a grand statue of a prominent man. He wears a grey, unbuttoned coat that appears to be stained because it has been there—sun and rain—for a long time.

To the eye of the casual observer, the relatively modest five-metre or so stone figure doesn't seem to be anything out of ordinary. A large plaque at the base reveals it "marks the site of another plaque" that presumably has been stolen. The captain got this one instead. Cook was kind of first—a "Bradbury" of the eighteenth century who raised his hand and coined the face to an unknown continent.

He was not the first, he was not the last. To better understand it, Australia has to be discovered time and time again. And ideally, there need to be crowds of discoverers.

Because here they are, the omnipresent images pinned to our subconscious repository of the Antipodean preconceptions: a kangaroo, a koala, intense goldish sunset on a blue horizon, face-painted Aboriginal people with boomerangs hopping around a fire for tourists, the Opera House, the Harbour Bridge, grinning students in marketing catalogues. Then money in excess, lunch breaks spent surfing at Bondi Beach and Santa—Santa-bloody-Clause in swimmers in the very middle of "winter".

Yeah. Stereotypes.

We're touching down. This time with no ovations.

2
Underdogs to Explorers

Before I went there, I had only met two Australians in the flesh and bone in my whole life. It's as if they had been in short supply, or the world had run out of them. Then, when I first arrive in Sydney, a whistling turbaned taxi driver with an accent totally unknown to me takes me from the airport to my first hostel. After finding out where I come from, he pauses his tune and utters, "Lendl. Nedved," then purses his lips again and carries on. The air is different—warm and wet, as if drawn from the sea—and there are strange noisy birds with even weirder squealing sounds everywhere. White parrots and brown ferals called miner birds.

I get used to Sydney more or less instantly; after a month I don't mind bus stop benches facing off streets to make it harder for me to see the arriving buses, cyclists notoriously ignoring red lights and water in taps so hot I can brew a coffee in it. The city icons, blah; its cultural life, blah, blah; the First State Metropolis. A big yawn. It's advertised everywhere.

Suddenly I am a part of that pulse, the grandeur. I am so cool, I am so in. I own everything around, yet nothing belongs to me. The skyscrapers' night silhouettes, pulsating shopping centres, the variety. As if all the world has somehow made it to this one place for me. Nevertheless, I can't wait for the triumphant moment when I challenge all that, and rewrite history with my own trip. But not just yet.

Cook must have been an incredible persona to reach a land so far away from his home on just a pile of nailed wooden planks with some sails affixed to them, having but a sextant as his main navigation tool. He kind of popped in by chance at that, after observing the transit of Venus— his main job. He was to check the unknown southern piece of land already spotted years ago by the Dutch and the French. So he did. Once he was here, though, all he had to do was to get off his ship.

He arrives as quite an extraordinary overseas explorer.

When I want to properly set foot on the continent, my status is figuratively teetering on a small dinghy still somewhere between Kuala Lumpur and Jakarta. Moreover, it sails right into a major storm. I can already sense the rising swell of the ocean. After about three months, I am coming to the conclusion that I don't own the continent at all; it is the continent that owns every inch of me.

I arrive as quite an ordinary overseas student.

Student visas and relating fees, exorbitant education costs, selective commercial insurance, unfunny agents living off my commission, astronomical rents, sleepless nights. The fourth month, my mind is already in a loop, thinking how to bust myself out of that vicious cycle and remain in sane spirit.

I go to the immigration office for advice. "G'day. Howsitgoin? Can you please give me some kind of a—writ—so that I can, just in the philosophical sense, roam free?"

I get a decent answer immediately. *Get lost*.

Or, *get used?* Something like that, because on seeing my distraught face, they call me *mate* and have my arms loaded with a huge stash of beautifully tinted forms so that in my free time from dusk to sunrise, I can read them, study them, fill them in and out, sign them, check them, provide more details, then read and study them again, fill in and sign them, recheck and send them one after another to authorised bureaucratic institutions.

After two centuries of British influence, Australia came out rather overregulated—but in saying that—in a very romantic way. While in many parts of Europe, the office rats would have long scratched your eyeballs out of the lateral rectus muscles for not filling out a form correctly, here the patient officers collect every detail, right down to the size, colour, and smell of your right sock, and you can even ask questions. They don't even have to think much. The system does it for them. For example:

"Hi, I lost my wallet and need new driver's licence."

"You must pay for a replacement."

"Yes. But I lost my wallet with everything in it."

"That's fine. You can pay by card."

"Yes. But I lost my wallet, and my cards were also in it."

"Okay, you can pay by cash then. There is an ATM around the corner—"

"Yes, but—". Anyway. If you don't have your IDs, you don't exist. The local euphemism for this is '100 points of identification checklist'. The only place where they do not require you to show identification, is at the polling booths where citizens vote at elections. The voters just point to their names on a long electorate roll and they're rewarded with a free non-permanent pencil with ballot paper and a question whether they—rascals—already didn't vote somewhere else on that day. If they say they didn't, they can copy a 'how to vote pamphlet' received from a volunteer of their choice in front of the entrance. The so called preferential voting system will then see to it that either the 'Red Party' or the 'Blue Party' will land a majority. With this wonderful mutual trust system in place, just about anybody can vote in Australia. But then, why would they? Don't they have better things to do?

There are stories of people whose identity was mismatched by the electoral computer system with persons who were already deceased but shared the same name and surname.

"I am sorry, you cannot vote because you are already dead," the poll officer said.

They had to go through the full identification conundrum in multiple institutions to prove that they were still alive.

And so, with each additional form filled, we are getting better and better acquainted with the local mentality, the Australian accent, form opinions about the local system of government, education, culture, work ethic, food, transport; what is driving the streets, what is all the rage on TV, and later on even memorise the name of the prime minister.

The last mentioned—or rather, one of his underlings—finally informs us, in a very special memorandum, that the government approved our expedition plans and from now on we can regard ourselves promoted in status—from alien subjects from another planet to a semi-domesticated breed of vassals who can freely roam but should not jump too high. They call it PR, which everywhere else stands for Public Relations, but here in Australia it means Permanent Residency. Yes, getting PRed is equivalent to taking off the proverbial chain iron ball from your right foot. And hey, you don't have to vote as a bonus.

In a short addendum inscribed at the bottom of the page, in rather tiny caps starting "Conditions Apply", the PM also informs us that while a new discovery expedition is encouraged, he's certainly NOT contributing a single bloody cent, let alone a dollar.

Fair enough.

And that leads us to the second concern. A financial one. If one is not a millionaire's brat, or you're not the Crown's choo choo boys, some kind of work will almost certainly be welcome.

We have nothing to lose and so we pack up and get a no-frills ticket to the opposite coast, as far as we can while we still have some cash. There, in Perth, WA, we'll try to resurrect ourselves from the dead and totter across Australia back to Sydney.

It's a five-hour flight, enough time to admire the endless beautiful plains, so flat that surely it's going to be a breeze to cross them. With a brand new toothbrush in the backpack, a few books, and a meagre debit card, we can't wait for the journey to start.

As a matter of fact, it has already started.

3
Everybody Can: No Pain No gain

"Do you have experience cleaning bogs, mate?"

"I beg your pardon?"

"What experience do you have cleaning toilets?" asks the bulky-looking Lebanese supervisor, who does a sort of recruitment while finishing his morning tea consisting of a fresh doughnut.

"Well, I—I did it—I did it once—at home—" I reply, somewhat surprised.

Wrong answer. High-level employment questions like that should be met with a wide smile, beaming enthusiasm and an assertion that cleaning *dunnies* has always been the most fulfilling part of my entire career, and it is something I definitely want to stay with until I retire. I'm just lovin' it.

"Yeah, you need the local experience."

Hell, aren't bogs the same everywhere? It's true that in North America and Taiwan, I sat on bowls full of big lake of water, and if the Tsar Bomba hit the surface from the wrong angle the resulting splash didn't mushroom from the toilet only because my bum acted as a cork stopper. Australia adopted the European system, like a small fishpond, the surface of which can additionally be camouflaged with a bit of toilet paper for gentler impact when your short-range ballistic missiles reach the target. In that regard I felt very much at home and couldn't see a problem.

If you abandon the official line and say something stupid like, "Um, I just need some dough to travel, mate," it won't work. It goes without saying for better jobs in particular.

It would be silly to think that with the PR 'domesticated alien' status we're going to rank as high as we used to back at home. Quite the contrary. It might be a serious ride down the career path, especially in the beginning. But who cares? Embrace it because short-term shitty jobs are excellent opportunities to experience the continent from its very bottom, as it were, and shouldn't that be on every true explorer's list? It provides a whole wealth of opportunities and invaluable insights.

Why would I want a high-flying job when I am going to quit after only a few weeks? It's like skipping the whole foreplay before making love out of habit, or arriving at a fancy restaurant, snubbing the entrée, the soup, the main dish and leaping right onto the sweet dessert, devouring it greedily and demonstratively burping in front of the entire floor.

Surely something will be missing. Skipping this crucial stage prevents you from getting the whole picture.

Kitchen hand will be a fantastic start!

The restaurant is run by an Indian guy called Paul. Paul, who can reliably distinguish between Danish and Norwegian because he used to work in Sweden, never has any supplies on stock until the very moment he takes an order. Once he knows what he needs, he hysterically starts to boss around his kitchen hand—me—who starts desperate rallies to the nearby shopping centres. "Quick! Quick! Go! Go! Before the table leaves!" Be it chicken breasts, cauliflower lettuce, veal, a plastic strainer or spatula because he has just broken one when killing a cockroach.

While that is being looked after, he proceeds to supervise his kitchen staff, occasionally unloading a parsley sprig from a used plate returned to the kitchen, and beautifully arranges it on top of a new plate that his American waitress is delivering to a customer.

"Savings matter, mate."

"How about the steaks? Did you get them too?" he asks me on my return. "Didn't Luke tell you we needed them?"

Luke, a plump naturalised English cook with an unshaven stubbled face, arrives at work about two hours late that morning because he got entangled in a pub brawl last night—quite innocently, of course. Standing between two local skips who dared question his Pom heritage, he thought this was an excellent opportunity to teach them a lesson or two about manners:

"Strewth, mate! Your bathroom home-brew's the best in the world, eh?" he mocked them in a poor imitation of their own accent.

All he remembers next are heavy boot soles walking all over his face. Two fresh brass-knuckle-carved grooves are stamped on his swollen cheeks, while a third adorns his nose along its full length. He can only see us through one of his eyes.

"Calling me a cunt and stomping my face didn't help them one fucking bit, mate," he still maintains through the bruised corner of his red mouth, going about his usual business.

Luke works in hospitality, which means if he's not dead, he has to show up. That, however, doesn't stop everybody wondering how on earth he is still able to stand. With Luke, the only plausible explanation is the legendary British stamina that has made it possible to inhabit a continent as inhospitable as Australia, and if not for him "none of you bloody losers would be around today". And he always has a good piece of fatherly advice at hand. "Go home, get some Steven Seagal movies, and beat the shit out of your girlfriend."

*The west coast of Australia is different in one particular way. Unlike the eastern states, the sun actually doesn't rise from the sea but from the land mass horizon, and beautifully illuminates the whole city of Perth in the morning.

A lady in a recruitment agency is going out of her way to assure me that every two minutes a new plane lands in WA, full of overzealous immigrants with only one objective—to take working opportunities away from me the moment they touch down. I shouldn't risk not accepting her offer. "You'll be a part of a cleaning squad and you cover all your working expenses. You'll get hourly rates and you need an ABN - Australian Business Number - as a prerequisite. You'll be a cleaning 'businessman'.

The cleaning of the conference rooms starts at four a.m., finishes at nine. By seven I am done and go home. I lie down in my makeshift bed and wake up at about noon. I open my eyes and my mind slowly starts to kick in. A hangover? I am not sure, but a few more bucks are landing in my bank account towards the end of the week.

If a better, more sophisticated job is at stake, one needs to pay particular attention to the CV, better known here as a résumé. It is a bit like breast augmentation: it needs to look good on the outside but what is really in it is far less important. A good first impression is what counts most if I get a chance, plus references from those who knew me from the past, boundless self-confidence and a strong desire to crown my life by pounding keyboards of a large corporation until death does us part. Then, after three months, I find it is totally and completely incongruent with my life philosophy of a nomad and I simply quit.

What follows is probably the most intense and spiritually rewarding educational phase of my life. A true crash course.

4
Crash Course in Australian Basic Education

The learning curve in a strange land is much steeper. It's a little bit like being born again and looking at the new world through the eyes of an innocent infant. The world seems to be familiar and is alleviated by instincts, but up until now I've been in my mother's womb without any real experience of life outside. I've been uncompromisingly pushed out, landing on big cold metal weighing scales. If I get a job, it will be a boob to suck on to grow and get bigger, with only one slight difference: instead of getting on my feet in two years, I will need to do it in two months. And in another six months, I'll have to go through a development cycle that normally takes ten years. Observation is my strongest weapon.

Cleaning a local public school, I learn "on the go". I read notice boards about reconciliation efforts between the indigenous and majority population—a topic that, together with racial tolerance, has been around for a few generations now, in the sense that the colonisers disposed the indigenous people of their cultural identity.

The next room is science. There is a large paper box with warm light inside, where new life is hatching from under the white fragile eggshells. At first they are round and full, but every day they crack more and more as their habitants try to reach daylight. The chooks will greet the world soon.

I become two years older in the next room. I learn about the solar system—Jupiter's diameter is eleven times larger than that of Earth—and read about lives of famous astronomers—Tycho Brahe is listed higher than Copernicus.

I observe a full range of fruits and veggies all across the floor, giving me a perfect idea of what had been on the menu today. Combined with piles of sand and lumps of dirt brought from the playground—it is not practical for kids to take their shoes off—and remnants of what once used to be writing tools and paper sheets, the picture of the school day is nearly complete.

My quiet contemplation is interrupted by a teacher. She has come back for some stuff she forgot when tidying up her desk, because from tomorrow she will be on her long service leave—a long paid holiday break after fifteen years of service. She is stopping in Bali and then going to Europe, which in the popular parley of many means somewhere *starting in England and ending in Germany, with France halfway in-between.*

"How about going around Australia?" I am curious.

"Far out! I wish I could do that. But I don't have time!" Australians tend to go overseas. "You probably know more about Australia than I do," she giggles.

To which I reply that I find locals very knowledgeable about both. Older generations mainly. An Australian friend of mine went for a tour of Iran without knowing anybody there. He just wanted to see the country. Despite common fears of hostility toward westerners, what he came across were the most hospitable and friendly people he has ever met, a beautiful ancient country with quite good, cheap inland airline connections. And he only spoke English at that. "What a disappointment for the official mainstream doctrine," he said. "Right now our prime minister is in America, doing a certain amount of sucking up to the Yanks". But this was the only thing he hated about his government. We met him in Slovakia, hiking in the mountains of High Tatras. when he noticed gypsies chopping firewood in a national park.

"Oh, they are like the Aborigines," he said.

5
Driving Thingybob and the Holy Licence

There is just one more thing to sort out before getting out the door: a valid local driver's licence, which is also an ID. If you happen to come from "the right" country, they will just swap it for an Aussie one. Otherwise, too bad. Once you are a permanent resident—a "domesticated alien"—you should stop using the overseas licence after a short period. Then you might need to go through another crash course. Getting used to the other side of the road.

Theory comes first. There is some practical stuff like drinking prevention: how many beers you can park and still hit the road? The answer is: Two for Wayne, one for Sheila. Equality hasn't reached this domain yet. Or questions like: when the road surface is wet, the braking distance required is' a) shorter b) same c) longer? The answer is: Longer. Or: why do you need to stop before a railway track? The answer: Because trains are heavy and take a long time to stop.

Australian traffic lights are on a 24/7 regime, which means all around the clock, seven days a week and fifty-two weeks a year. If by any miracle they ever stop flashing, this kind of situation is so unusual, nobody seems to recall the 'give way to the right rule'. For a few minutes, it becomes Thailand. All cars, no matter where they are, stop so drivers can scratch their heads. As long as the stream of cars on the main road is winning, all who are in it happily chug along until one of the cars on the adjacent road is bold enough to push through. Then the cars behind it follow suit until one of the braver drivers on the other road finds a gap and forces the cycle back where it started. And so it goes on until police arrive because of an accident. They don't exactly have to run the intersection by now because the company in charge of the traffic lights has already fixed the traffic computer. The lights are back in action.

Back to the driver's licence. One can get an international version of an overseas driving licence that can be used for some time in Australia, but they look rather dodgy. The police officer presented with such a document during a routine road check—usually a folded worn-down A5 brochure in French—will raise his eyebrows and mumble something to the effect of, "What the hell is this?"

If I need to go for a driving test in New South Wales, I need to show up in a car. Now, how can I arrive in my own car, if in theory I don't have a local driving licence? A bit of a catch-22 to foreigners but never mind. There are plenty of car rentals. One-day rates are relatively expensive and so it's better to rent it for a few days and combine it with a nice trip after the exam.

Once I have booked the exam and rented the car, I arrive to the organisation in charge of traffic management. It's a different organisation in each state and it keeps changing regularly every three to five years thanks to the government's committment to 'continuous improvement'. After filling in some forms and showing some papers like insurance for the car I've just hired, my driver's licence translation and payment card details, I am escorted to the vehicle by an officer wearing a shiny yellow-orange vest. He casually asks how I am—something that is compulsory here—but he looks like he couldn't care less. For the next half-an-hour or so he is going to assess my driving skills. He is going to meticulously tick all the boxes on his checklist. And I don't blame him—he has been here since the morning, my driving test is about his sixth, for the fourth day in a row he has been annoyed by rookies who know bugger-all about changing gears, overtaking, backing up, parking, who stomp the gas pedal too abruptly, brake too violently, don't look in the rear-view mirror, passionately cuddle the steering wheel and what's worse: enter the wrong side of the road. Of course, that's not me. I've already driven about two thousand kilometres in Australia and New Zealand by now!

Some mistakes are considered minor, only reducing my score, while others will be punished by almost a certain fail. The officer needs to tick them all. While performing a three-point-turn in a narrow lane somewhere on the city outskirts, I'm halfway through the test.

The officer only gives me his judgement from the safety of his chair behind the counter, shielded by a thick glass window. He is prints a certificate.

"Mate, you didn't pass," he says calmly. Apparently I went both too fast and too slow and I didn't let go a car from the opposite direction when turning right, even though it was in another lane. He takes out a pair of large pliers and punches a half-inch hole in my overseas licence while issuing a the 'Learner' licence in an act of consolation.

"From now on you must wear a big 'L' on the car and you can only drive with somebody who has a full licence," sounds his advice.

"How am I going to get the car back to the rental company?" I ask.

"Well, you need somebody with a full licence."

I don't know anybody—with a full licence. In fact, I don't know *anybody* in here.

In two weeks, the same rental company willingly lends me the same car using the same old licence, although now visibly and officially "holey". An average Australian rental assistant doesn't give a flying duck about holes in overseas driver's licences.

There is a queue at the testing centre counter. An argument is going on between the officer in a yellow-orange vest and a young aspiring driver from Asia. The latter has just been told he failed.

The same officer with an equally bored expression greets me from the other side. It's down to formalities: driver's licence, car details, insurance, etc.

"Who drove you in, mate?" he asks casually with his eyes scanning the forms.

"A friend," I say.

"Sure," he replies, slightly annoyed.

We leave the garage and I am taken on a completely different route than the last time. The officer's strained look does not bode well.

From the safety of his chair he informs me I failed. This time, he says, I almost ran over a pedestrian.

"Who's taking you home? A friend ay?"

6
Indigenous Versus Conventional: Take I

When it comes to history, there is this one peculiar oddity: Australians don't seem to know with a hundred per cent certainty whether their ancestors discovered their own country or not. The stories are full of this pioneer and that pioneer first having come upon this spot and that place, saw that promontory first and explored that cove and mapped something else: noble grand discoveries. We came, we saw, we claimed.

Then—in 1988—there was a big celebration to commemorate bicentenary after the arrival of the Phillip's First Fleet and they needed to re-enact that event in a pompous show, also using Aboriginal performers, and this was to be for the eyes of the entire world. And one can imagine the poor choreographer handing out the parts.

"Now you people here are going ashore with oxen and sheep, the next group—men with heavy boxes, hens, grain, corn, the guards follow with convicts over there—" then he turns to a bunch of native actors recruited for the purpose, "—and you guys are going to welcome us from the shore with your spears and then you're going to—"

"That wasn't a welcoming gesture—" retorts somebody from that crowd suddenly.

"—pardon?"

"That wasn't a 'hi'. We wanted you to disappear, TO GET THE HELL OUT OF HERE!"

"Well—that's a—bit of a—diversion from the line—" he stutters, puzzled, putting his specks on to consult the script.

Then somebody even bolder at the back of the group shouts:

"It was an invasion! We've been here for fifty thousand years!"

And so, that is the exact moment that voice was finally heard and cast some doubts on the discovery claim. And hey, can't you and I discover Australia now too?

But then, if not discovery, what was is? Yes, there was violence, guns, the lot. But technically it doesn't live up to the whole picture. An army is usually invading something, but there was none. They even brought their own slaves. A 'friendly invasion' then, or a 'late discovery' maybe? An 'undiscovery'? Argh! I am totally confused. What was it? I want to know! One thing is quaranteed. Anything you say on this topic, one of the sides will always offer you a long stern look:

"Mate, you're so full of it".

A lawyer friend of mine wanted to save me from my frustration once and—over a beer—offered an explanation in the form of two seemingly unrelated stories. The first one starts in 1770 when Cook first sets foot on the local soil and the second one—about two hundred years later—when a person named Eddie Koiki Mabo feels the royal moccasin on his shoulder blade. Below are very laid-back, heavily lightened up, slightly convoluted pub versions of both stories mixed up in one.

7
The Case Nullius and Terra Mabo

When the famous English globetrotter James Cook descended from his boat in New Holland in 1770, it was one of his many amazing discoveries. Apart from noticing numerous queer animals, which were hastily painted on parchment by his associates, he couldn't help noticing some very strange men as well. They were unclad and they didn't respond to his interpreter, whose language skills up to this point had got them nicely along the whole Pacific:

"Aloha!"

No response.

"Aloha! Aloha!"

Nothing.

The natives threw a few baffled looks at one another, stood up, and taking their wooden spears, slowly walked away. After several futile attempts at communication, Cook continued to observe them, finally concluding that savages lived within very modest means, they had neither shelters nor fences and that he was in *terra nullius*—no man's land—an empty uncivilised country not owned by anyone.

The absence of fences in particular was taken as a noteworthy observation. Later that evening, the Union Jack was erected and Cook, pressing his foot against the seashore rock, observed a romantic sunset. With his elbow resting on his knee, and looking through his binoculars into the far sea beyond, in solemn contemplation he opened his lips and just for himself whispered a never recorded sequence of words: "If it's not theirs, whose is it?"

Nearly two hundred years later, an indigenous activist—except he didn't know he was one yet—was making his way home from work. Eddie Koiki Mabo was an ordinary man living in Murray Island in Queensland's Torres Strait. He had happily inhabited his small shack for many years and enjoyed a quiet and humble life with all the simple pleasures the Crown had to offer to the loyal subjects in the subdued domains. "Today is today and tomorrow is tomorrow. A little smile can save the day no matter what", and he didn't give a damn about politics, trusting only what he could see right in front of his eyes.

One day, a rainforest pigeon delivered him a letter with a beautiful official stamp portraying a chic lady sporting a necklace. The last sentence of it plainly informed him that within two years, a brand new multi-lane fancy road was going to be whizzing through the middle of his humpy's living room.

"None of that! Over my fucking dead body!" he shouted, and in the sudden thrust of emotion he proceeded tearing the document to pieces, at the same time fiercely waving off swarms of annoying flies from his sweaty neck.

"Fucking government!" he snorted. "You're not getting away with that! I am doing something about it! NOW!" And he did. He went to a local pub and got plastered.

And as he was leaning against the bar, giving the bored bartender his story, it caught the ear of a stranger, a gentleman sitting at the nearby table.

"Pardon me, gentlemen," he said, "perhaps I can help. I know a bit about America and how they've already dealt with the problem there." And he went on to a lengthy description of the ordeals the Native Americans had to go through.

"—and with this, they had to prove they had their own law and the paleface had trespassed that law. The court eventually accepted the notion and their claim to the stolen land became legitimate. You have to go down the same path."

Despite a headache in the morning, Eddie sought the mysterious scholar again.

"You need to prove you had some kind of rules to govern yourselves, some kind of a code that the British have violated. You might have scribbled it down somewhere, leather, rocks, stones, trees?"

"I don't know," he replied politely.

"Something you used to rule your lives, maintain peace and order; some—you know—some customary law you had passed on from generation to generation and wrote down somewhere, anything! Anything?"

"We only painted," he said, and then to make his point clearer he added: "We never wrote."

The professor took off his glasses and rubbed his temples.

"Well, then we have a problem."

He visited Mabo again in a month's time.

"Even if you didn't write anything, somebody else might have. Wasn't there anybody else who wrote something down for you?"

Eddie thought. He remembered his grandfather saying once that his parents had met some very strange people. They liked to share everything and they read from a big book and asked questions that nobody could answer. "They laughed at us, saying an octopus couldn't be God and..."

"The missionaries! That's it!" exclaimed the prof in joy. "They wrote. And they wrote a lot! We really have to find those manuscripts."

Neither of them had the faintest idea then they had just started a ten-year journey through the labyrinth of lawsuits.

The main and most crucial point of the whole dispute was to prove that the aboriginal people owned their lands in the true sense, which is described as Native Title to Land. It wasn't easy, but in the end it was upheld by court in a breakthrough decision.

Mabo, however, didn't live to see the final verdict. Without ever knowing it, he managed to win the most significant precedent in the legal history of Australia. It was named after him: the Mabo Case.

From around 1992, the natives were able to lay claims to regain their 'stolen' lands and the disputes were very complex. The government has withheld the right to lands that were acquired 'legally' in compliance with the anti-discrimination laws of the 70s. The trials took six years in average and many claimants didn't live to see the end. What was left in most cases was mainly desert and wasteland of little value. The lucrative lands like green pastures, parts of towns or areas with mineral deposits in the possession of big business and corporations were already untouchable.

In a gesture that costs nothing, the natives are often called 'traditional custodians of the land' during public events in spite of the fact that they have no rights to those lands and not a remote chance of ever getting them back.

Loved and hailed by politicians and public officials who use the acknowledgement before their speeches and meetings, while treated as a cynical and cheap virtue-signalling act by others, the so called 'Welcome to Country' became part of Australian culture. The 2023 Australian Indigenous Voice referendum will show however that an absolute majority of Australians do not wish to be welcomed in their own country.

Nevertheless, Mabo changed Australia like no other before him. The conservative part of Australia tried to overturn the precedent, but it could no longer be undone.

Three years after Mabo's death, an unknown perpetrator desecrated his tomb. Mabo was buried again in his native Murray Island, this time like a king.

8
Hatch, Hatch, Hatchback

The Australian travel equation is simple—one and one are two, but no matter what, we need to be prepared and have three things ready: One. Water—always and everywhere. Two. A head cover and sun protection, also always and everywhere, because sunstroke isn't our friend and every European newcomer looked at least once like a sizzled sausage when underestimated the Australian sun.

And finally, three. Spare tyre and a toolbox with equipment, whether or not we plan to go far beyond the main roads. We can't prepare for the unpredictable, of course, but we can at least minimise possible trouble.

Should we want to go north, the so called 'winter' months will be more suitable for it. They start in June.

Winters and summers in Australia are very different from those in the northern hemisphere. "Freezing' temperature in Australia is generally agreed to be about +13 degrees Celsius. Many people in winter simply crawl out of their houses to rest on the sun like reptiles because many houses have insufficient insulation, single-pane windows and tiled roofs with no sarking. Some people still use electric blankets in winter and many these days cannot imagene life without air conditioning. If a house has a northern aspect it means it gets northern sun which is regarded as an extra feature.

Additionally, the north of the country is completely different from the south. In the north the winter season is better known as the dry season and the summer is known as the wet season. What one person in Darwin describes as 'cold', another person in Adelaide would call 'positively balmy'.

The weather patterns can, however, be thrown out of sync completely. One might get stuck on the road because of floods or fires just about any time. Then the roads are closed or blocked without any regard to your travel plans.

As for the infrastructure, only larger city centres evolved before the great invention of car. So if you live and work there, public transport will do, unless you are keen on spending half of your pay on parking fees and fines. However, if you need to be mobile and flexible somewhere out there—outside of big city conglomerates— a car will be an absolute must. Since the 1950s, towns and cities have been shaped and designed just for them. Australia is one of a few countries in the world where people use their cars as shoes leaving them in caparks and then walking barefooted among freezers in grocery stores.

There is only one thing in Australia I cannot do in public: Wearing socks in sandals, because it's like hanging a big sign from my neck in capital letters saying: *I AM A WEIRDO FROM OVERSEAS*.

So what cars are there to choose from? There is plenty.

"You're going to travel, mate?" asks a young pumped-up sales rep at a second-hand car dealership.

"Well, first I'd like to—"

"—you need a BIG station wagon, mate," he says in a say-no-more tone. He stretches his hand and says, "It's going to be your house for the next few months, you know what I mean? This is what you need, look no further, it's a bargain."

I look around not convinced.

"Can I take it for a test drive to a car mechanic nearby? I'd be back in an hour. If it's okay, I'll buy."

Two previous ones said no. This one says yes and will hold my driver's licence as deposit so he knows I am coming back. If I am pulled up by police, I simply tell them he has got my licence and everything will be sweet. "That's normal, here" he says.

The car mechanic shakes his head. "No bloody way, mate. The gearbox is leaking, that's the downside of this model. If it comes apart while you're on the road, nobody is going to piece it together.

The aircon doesn't work anyway. Look, buy something reliable, even small, without aircon. When I was young, there were no bloody aircons and we lived. Toyota. You might pay a few extra bucks but it retains value once you want to get rid of it."

We return the big old Ford. "Very good car. But no thank you." We can't buy it yet anyway. In fact, we're still waiting for money from the rental bond in Sydney. We are hunting Toyotas for the next two days. The more time it takes, the more stress descends on us. We'll get a trouble to get to work without a car and if we don't have a job we won't have enough money to buy a car soon. One mistake and we're broke.

We've spent the last week staying with an Australian friend we once met in Europe.

"Be careful. All car dealers are criminals. Every bloody one of them," he says. "Take your time, don't let them push you into a buy. TAKE YOUR TIME."

Sure, will do. Three more days and we finally have it. A white fifteen-year-old Corolla with the odo proudly showing 485,548 km on the dashboard. We have a tyre, oil and light bulb changed. That's always advised before handing the money. With a small daily limit on the card, we need two instalments: that is, two days to pay. No problem.

"You can borrow this old treasure and come back tomorrow with the balance."

Holden—the Australian equivalent of Opel, Vauxhall or the banal GM—has this one last task to do before it will inevitably fall apart hopefully before we return it.

Meanwhile, sadly, our interim host loses it as we have come home late for the second time in a row. After all, we 'took our time' following his advice. But he has an excellent solution. Why don't we disappear tomorrow first thing in the morning? All of a sudden the car surly becomes a house. Not for long, though, because there is this next job we need to do.

9
Slowly, Slowly Catchee Possum

The right moment for the journey hasn't arrived yet. We are going north and ideally we need to start around June.

For the next few months we're going to house-sit a fibro cottage at the fringe of Perth called Forrestdale. And not just the house. We'll have a dog and three large cats to look after; not knowing whether we're minding them or they're minding us, in this flat middle of nowhere.

All cats boast different personalities. Tom Cat thinks he is a dog. He likes to be walked. Fat Cat is asleep all day, with a few meal breaks in between. And Pocket Cat vanishes in the morning and returns at night with her stomach full of local fauna. The German Shepherd called Zsa Zsa barks in Hungarian because her owner comes from Budapest. Her husband, in turn, is from South Africa and he is fluent in German, English, Afrikaans and Zulu. One day he gave up, and like many thousands of his countrymen, packed up and went to Australia. He brought and sold a yacht—one of unofficial ways to get the money out of the country.

So we now live in this house shrubs around it and fetch fresh raw kangaroo mince from a local farm outlet every day. The meat looks like salami—apparently the highest quality pet food in the world. The nearest bus stop is a good few kilometres away; we can't see the nearest neighbour, only his fence and his donkey, who goes by the name of Elvis.

Not all houses are like that, but in this one you can hardly breathe in the summer heat, and almost exhale steam in winter when the temperatures drop close to freezing. This somehow funny, flimsy, low budget, botched construction is quite popular. Saving on utility bills is not exactly a thing yet.

There is a big ostrich farm nearby. An ostrich, unlike its Australian cousin, the emu, is an import from Africa. He is unpredictable. It's not a good idea to get anywhere near. He can rip you open with his mighty claws—probably a dormant, intrinsic feat inherited from dinosaurs. One of his huge eggs equals twenty those from a chook, and the plenty of pancakes made from one of them will feed the whole party of swearing bricklayers.

It is a strange feeling to be in this semi-seclusion. As if near a city, yet still far beyond. Only a few kilometres from here there is a new urban sprawl, and it's coming closer and closer every day, like plague. What were once inhospitable plains now belong to the fast-growing satellite towns behind tall soundproof barriers, with large shopping malls not far apart, reachable only by cars, wide streets and further infrastructure that in Perth is built systematically on huge budgets. There's also a small lake, at least on a local map. In reality it's an inaccessible muddy swamp with diverse vermin all around it.

The house roof gutters are full of redbacks—small spiders with a red dot on their backs—probably the most notorious leader of the arachnophobia charts. People like to mention redbacks to impress family members and friends by saying how close to death they were when taking rubbish bins out on their holidays in Australia Or after having one too many, as *Red Back* is also one of the local beer brands. With a little knowledge and prevention, the spider is harmless. Sweeping roof gutters with a broom, for instance, is a no-no because when they fall down to the ground, they can bite if stepped on. We walk in shoes, no matter how hot it is. And it *is* hot. Apparently, a tradie got bit on the willy once while reading a newspaper on a toilet seat, and there is even a song about it. In the song, his wife wants to help him with a knife but he objects the cure might be worse than the disease.

Western Australia has more mineral wealth than all the countries of Western Europe combined, and it is the de facto richest state. Some die-hard West Ozzies love to comment sarcastically, with a noticeable dose of patriotism and a visible sneer, "God bless the desert, separating us from the eastern states. We can do without them but they can't do without us."

Fremantle is a small town at the start of the Inner Harbour.

Unlike the fast-growing city of Perth, Freo has European charm with low-pitched buildings and narrow streets. In one way, it's like the nearby Northbridge, a suburb, with better nightlife than in the Perth CBD, where after sunset everything clears out faster than a swimming pool with a Polly Waffle in it. Not that we want to know much about night life now. We're in saving mode. We get up brutally early and the mere thought of it is keeping us awake, despite the fatigue.

Now and then a bird screeches so loud it might be taken for a human voice. A sound orgy just a few yards from the windows. With so many birds, a few kinds are squealing so loudly it can seriously damage the delicate ligaments of the permanently underslept nervous system. Once I swear I even heard an imitation of my alarm clock coming back from the bush. There are birds that can immitate it like the lyrebird although rarely spotted. Others, like the kookaburra—a large kingfisher type of a bird with a long beak—can laugh, in a truly hysterical chitter.

As for other native animals, possums are noteworthy because they are a bit like a cross between squirrel and cat. The squirrelcats love to invade garbage bins, with quite some noise, and they come down from trees at night, stop and stare into your torch without movement. Then they disappear in less than a second. While they are endangered protected larrikins on Australian soil, no animal on earth would possibly want to be a possum in New Zealand, where the only use for them are decorative furs.

Today we're getting up at quarter past two in the morning. We have to be there at three. It's the first cleaning shift. With eyes glued to the steamed morning window, I start driving towards the city in complete darkness. It's rather cold. The traffic lights at Freo intersection signals amber. Will I make it or not? At night it is often endless waiting: one car halted on red versus no traffic at all. Sure will. Except that the white Holden behind starts to strobe like a disco in the eighties. He immediately pulls up.

In the rear-view mirror, I see a hulk of an officer getting out of his car.

"Good morning," I say, as if this wasn't going to provoke him even more. It's only five to three.

"Do you have driver's licence at all, mate?"

"Yes," I say and hand it out, saying nothing more. He takes it slowly and studies it patiently.

"This was issued in New South Wales," says the guy after a while.

"Yes."

He walks around the car, then returns.

"It wasn't amber, mate, it was red," he says slowly.

"I'm sorry. I was in a hurry," I say. I can't think of anything better.

Now I am only waiting for execution. *Coup de grâce*.

"Where are you going?" he asks.

"Work. Esplanade Hotel." New estimates start immediately to feed my database of fines. It's not the first one.

"Mate. You'll go real slow now, never cross red again and have your driver's licence changed for the local one. Have a good day."

10
Pavlova

In 1929, one of the world's best-known prima ballerinas, Anna Pavlova, was on a tour around Australia. On her way home, after performances in the eastern states, she called in on Fremantle's Esplanade Hotel. She was exhausted. Australia had different rail gauges in each state and she'd had to carry her bags a few times from one train to another. She even carried a couple of birdcages with her.

She sailed to Perth this time and didn't forget about her little vice: a sweet tooth. Yes, strange. She was a ballerina. Despite being a world-class performer, in every port she visited, all around the world, she ordered sweet cakes. It was no different in Fremantle. The cook must have parted the previous night, only arriving in the small hours of the morning, tired. The slightest sound was like a heavy hammer pounding at his forehead. "Sweet cake for the ballerina."

"Sweet cake for the ballerina!" the special order stated.

"What cake?" he asked.

"Cake, cake," was the answer. "How am I supposed to know?" says the other voice in an insistent tone. "A cake. But quick. She doesn't have much time."

With his left hand supporting his heavy head, he reached for a bowl into which he instinctively threw a few egg whites. He added a pinch of salt and went on thinking about the previous night, while whipping, whipping and whipping, after which he started to pour sugar. The morning light from the window was entering his half-open eyes with an inverted image that was slowly being put back on its feet inside his brain.

"Come on, mate! Miss Pavlova is waiting," a voice demanded.

When he came to, the mixture of egg whites and sugar were a white, thick consistency. He added more *sugar*, vanilla *sugar*, *suga-*

*r*again and vinegar topped with *sugar*. Then he quickly chucked it in the oven. When it came out, he couldn't believe his eyes. He disguised the white pile with sweet fruits, the more the better, topping it with some whipped cream to fill the cracks.

A new recipe was born: Pavlova.

But of course, all that is a total and complete lie because the ballerina had had a similar experience in New Zealand around that time. So who does she belong to now? Nobody knows.

Sadly, she died young, only a few years later, but in a way, she lives on. Pavlova—the legend.

11
Off Ya Go

A car breakdown somewhere in the middle of nowhere can represent quite a serious problem if I am not a Top Gear star with a logistics team of professionals and a camera crew in tow. The former would quickly repair it and the latter would make it look like I fixed it myself.

There are many car wrecks along the long road stretches that didn't survive trips. Their once proud owners did not bother fixing or towing them, and left them behind like unwanted puppies after Christmas. Too expensive. Rusty, derelict, often burnt down vehicle torsos: that is the fate of cars that don't make it. It translates to the wallet as well. Buying another car somewhere—and new equipment, because everything had to be left a few hundred kilometres behind after somebody gracefully gave us a lift. One can consider himself lucky if there's enough space in somebody else's car. That's the worst-case scenario. If something like that happens, incredibly large amount of time is lost. And what was to be a great adventure suddenly turns into unnecessary stress.

A well-prepared car is really important. At least in a few crucial points. Air conditioning should not be the main aspect when choosing it. There is a myth about Australia that it's hot, hot and hotter and you'll die if you don't fan yourself with cold air all day. When on the move, the open windows will do the job just as well. On the contrary, it can be surprisingly cold. Before setting out, it is critical that the engine has the cam belt—also known as the timing belt—changed. If it the belt gives out on the road, we're only a little bit less than screwed. The repair will cost much more. A preventive change of the engine seal won't hurt either. It is highly recommended to check the oil level when the engine is cold before starting every morning. If the engine burns out, the car is a write-off and so is a significant part of our journey. The engine will often start in the morning and stop at sunset and when we open it, it will literally be boiling. So make sure the cooling system works. Tyres are another must. Good onse will pay off.

And so will a good spare tyre and air pump, or the so-called "tyre seal" as the last resort. Petrol stations are every 100 to 200 kilometres, often more. If you go off the sealed roads, that distance gets longer and petrol gets more expensive. The further from civilisation, the dearer the fuel. Fuel stations in the outback are often in roadhouses, sometimes called homesteads, and they are grouped collections of buildings with a small grocery store and dust and flies hovering above its counters.

If you use a tent, the size of the car is irrelevant. Organising things inside it, however, is crucial It's advisable to have a good system, because after a month it will look exactly like the interior of a Russian tank in the final battles of the Second World War. The red dust is not such a problem as long as you know where things are. A knife or an opener or key disappearing somewhere down the trunk might mean hours of delay or worse, a toxic chain of events. For instance, in an attempt to make up for the time lost, we might forget to close the fuel tank and the lid—that rested on the roof—goes with you until you lose it in the roadside ditch many kilometres down the road. You won't buy a spare one in the next homestead. Junkyards and spare part stores will be thousands of kilometres away. It's also a good idea to have a second set of car keys. It sounds crazy, but a small distraction and a small mistake can turn your day into a nightmare.

We only used a spare fuel tank once. It is not as necessary as the drinking water canister; that must be topped up whenever possible. Before breaking camp each day, we get familiar with the road. We make each day's distances even and realistic.

Driving in Australia is tiring and so we allow for a lot of breaks. We take it easy. The kilometres ahead will not run away. It is a good idea to set off well after sunrise and stop well before sunset, avoiding driving at dawn and dusk. The omnipresent kangaroos love to go and check the road during that time. The risk of hitting them rises significantly. So let's say at 8 or 9 am we pack up and start, then in the afternoon, at about 4 to 5 pm, we start looking for a place to stay. There are many so-called rest places, rest areas or simply spots where one can stop for free without bothering anybody.

Town bookstores offer travel literature listing places like that. There are many titles that provide detailed road breakdowns. We can either write them down or just buy the book. That investment will pay for itself in no time. We are after twenty-four-hour rest places that are free. But even if they're not marked as 'twenty-four hour restplace', we can still stay overnight. Tiredness is our enemy and having a good rest is a must. Nobody will chase us away if we're tired except overzealous rangers in popular national parks. We are going to meet other 'explorers' there—in cars big and small, young cash-strapped in tents, fat bored retired owners of caravans, loners on motorcycles, dreamers and activists, adrenaline seekers on pushbikes of various shapes, hippy enthusiasts in strange vans and derelict cars, joggers and other extreme sports maniacs but also a handful of normal ordinary travelers. We will also meet locals.

If we happen to be there alone and the place looks dodgy, we wait. If nobody shows up, we just go on to the next one—that is why we need to start looking early. They are usually about fifty kilometres apart. Birds of a feather flock together and most travellers get settled in about one to two hours before sunset.

Australian soil is often so hard you can hardly pitch the tent in it. Having a good hammer might be a good idea. Even if the ground is nice and soft, we haven't won yet. There are often grass thorns called bindies, and so good mattresses will also help. When I am relieving myself in the dark shrubs at night, I don't forget about cobwebs. Especially in the north, Golden Orb Spiders—a huge, hairy bugger—lives between tree limbs and in shrubs. Rubbing it off the face in a half-asleep mode does not stand out in any list of pleasures.

We always tighten the tent firmly to the ground or any solid structure. We might enjoy watching stars and contemplating a cloudless night, and still get blown away by heavy wind by the morning. In these modern times, phone cards are history and only God Almighty—and Telstra, Australia's biggest and most pompous operator—know what has become of the phone booths in the outback. Have some coins and cash on you. If not for the phone, you will need it to pay for bush camps and they don't take credit cards. Believe it or not, they don't have any ATMs on the spot either. These places are in the middle of the bush. You're asked to throw money in an envelope and leave it in a box, ready for the rangers to pick it up next day. Satellite phones? Nah, that's ridiculous. We are explorers!.

It is a good idea to always have large plastic bags—the ones used for rubbish bins for different uses. In showers we wear *thongs*, which in Australia aren't bikinis with a narrow strap between the legs but rather a pair of flip flops. Showers we encounter in the outback aren't exactly what we call five-star. Usually they are no stars at all and less. It doesn't take great imagination to picture what's going on in there.

And the last thing: we try not to lose our cool under any circumstances. Firmly screw your head to the rest of the body and keep it there at all times.

II. Perth to Broome

12
At the Bottom of the Sea: Pinnacles

"Don't trust everything you read. A map is a good thing but never mistake it for the terrain," says Eman, our eighty-seven-year-old friend. He knows what he is talking about. He spent his life working for the Bata Shoe Company in different countries of the world like Kenya and Uganda, later India and Bangladesh, managing factories of a few thousand employees. He retired in Australia.

There are a few open travel guides on the table. The size of Australia hits home on a detailed map. It's comparable to the entire European continent from its very eastern fringes of Ural to Lisbon on the other side. The nearer the mountain, the steeper it seems.

The distance can be felt right on the first stretch from Joondalup to the sandstone formation of Pinnacles in the Nambung National Park. The Brand Highway takes about three hours and doesn't have many overtaking lanes. For a good hour we are driving through a pine forest that is rather a huge tree plantation. But in Australia many other plants are grown that way. The folks just learned to use the huge open spaces to yield something useful out of them and you occasionally come across them.

When we turn left off the highway called number one, in the western direction on Bibby Road, it is a long span going toward the ocean—a wide-open stretch.

The horizon shows itself a few times until the small town of Jurien Bay. There is white sand along the sides, but shortly before the iconic park it turns yellow. Nambung National Park[1] is not large but this one is like no other. It is better known as Pinnacles because there are these "pins" sticking out of the ground. Thousands of them.

When the first seafarers were exploring the Western coast of Australia, they noticed strange formations—thousands of stiletto-shaped rocks strewn across a relatively large area, grandly sticking out of the yellow ground, often as high as three metres. Apparently they first reminded them of ruins, but only much later they realised they were purely natural. The formation made of limestone shells is a seabed gone dry. It's been exposed to sun, rain and wind for thousands of years.

The Pinnacles: Nambung National Park

There is a tiny sandy road making its way around natural sculptures of different sizes and shapes. It is a one-way road. Yes, even national parks have them now. The area is just too large to be walked on foot. The sun lends the rock and sand exceptional colours. Pinnacles are iconic.

The evening sky in Jurien Bay looks promising. Another sunny day in sight, we think. It is very interesting how the land changes going north from there. Up to Geraldton there are dozens of large farms, thousands of acres of land with hundreds of cattle and even more sheep, huge green-and-yellow spaces, laced with dried out tree-tops, some of them a result of ring-barking —a technique used to clear land of lush trees: with a ring cut around their circumference, they will simply die without the need to cut them down. Easier. There are crosses along the road too—silent reminders that even an empty straight road can be treacherous. Very treacherous in fact because it lulls the senses to sleep and that is never good.

Every now and then we cross a cattle grid that is often marked with the yellow *Slow Down* road sign. Cows don't like to walk on uneven surfaces and so the grid serves a natural barrier, a kind of a fence in the ground.

Otherwise regular landscape, reminding us of Europe at times, is disturbed by *defects*—patches of land that refused to succumb to the agricultural obsession of the modern-day settlers, who tried to carve the landscape to their image. Those parts as if openly resisted and keep its wild and unkempt character. The further north, the more irregularities and the longer they are, until they become barren land entirely. Near Binnu, not far from Geraldton, farms are disappearing from sight and the dryness is getting the upper hand. Here somewhere the more isolated parts of Western Australia begin. There is a *Free Coffee for Driver* sign from time to time. It is a volunteer-run program to reduce fatigue-related accidents. It is certainly better to stop and sip coffee than be scraped off a tree at the nearest turn. Are you tired? Then don't wait. Stop! That's the message. The road starts to be very long indeed.

We stop at a twenty-four-hour rest place. There is a beautifully clear sky with thousands of stars in the evening. There are no lights around. What a fantastic weather we have got. Lucky us. Such an easy country to travel. That's exactly the moment we should have touched wood.

But we didn't.

13
Spider from Nerren Nerren

Nerren Nerren rest place is about 100 metres from the main road where heavy trucks roar all night. The place is among bushes and we have to set up the tent on a very hard gravel surface. There are wooden shelters. We tie our tent to one of them not knowing yet how wise this would later prove. In the middle of the night, strong gusts of wind wake us up. They come and go, regularly returning each time we fall asleep. The wind gradually increases to the point that the tent canvas almost wraps around our bodies, then springs back to its shape. After the breathtaking Pinnacles, this is like a cold shower in the middle of the night. Which for that matter comes right after.

In the morning a huge spider sits on the inside mesh of the tent. Rather crude awakening. It's about three inches wide and it's hairy. It was looking for a shelter and it has found one.

Huntsman spider on a tent mesh

In 1981 a person by the name of Gordon Wheatley tried to change a blown-out light globe in his house and stepped on something that he first thought was a pin. In fact he stepped on the most venomous spider in the world: the Sydney funnel-web spider. Only a year earlier a child died from its bite. What followed were the most frightening several hours of his life—his nervous system in a storm, his blood pressure doubled, his hands cramped and his lungs shrank uncontrollably. Yellow substance came out of his mouth and the doctor read 100 beats per minute His lungs started to fill with water. Dr Malcolm Fisher tells Mrs Whitley that her husband will be the first man in the world taking a newly-developed antibody. He didn't have a choice really. His heart rate was still rising. The first dose did nothing. He was served another one with no improvement still. Then the third one was administered but the patient was in agony.

The doc picked up the phone and called his friend. Struan Sutherland who had spent fifteen years of his life developing an antivenom. The development was sabotaged by bureaucrats, whose main job description was cutting public funds for research. Yet with increadibe patience he managed to develop a highly specialised technique of milking spider venom. Now, at half past one in the morning, somebody was yelling at him that his antidote was good for nothing.

"The stuff doesn't work! This is the third dose now! What do I do?," says the doctor.

"Well, give him more, I suppose." The doc hangs up.

An hour later, the phone rings again.

"It doesn't work! What should I do now?"

A short silence.

"If that didn't kill him—give him some more. Give him more."

The patient started to improve. The famous antidote now works with ninety-seven per cent success rate and the breakthrough hit medical journals. Since that day, no other spider-inflicted fatality in Australia has been recorded.

Huntsman sitting on our tent is a rather harmless and useful creature despite his horrible look. In fact, he looks like a crab, which is why he is also dubbed the giant crab spider. Most often you meet him sitting on walls, paitently waiting for pray that he hunts down with speed and precision rather than using web.

He likes posing for pictures and you can even place him in a plastic box for observation. He can dismantle a cockroach in the matter of minutes. Just never kill a huntsman spider. He wouldn't kill you. He is a friend. We're packing the tent and he goes his own way.

14
Pouring Buckets: Monsoon Rain

Up until now we don't know a monsoon rain means. There is a drizzle in the morning. Nothing much really. Surely it's going to stop as soon as we pack up, we're thinking. But it won't. It won't stop the whole day. It won't stop tomorrow, the day after tomorrow, not even after then. The road becomes wet and monotonous. There are bushes all along it; often you can't see what's behind them. Here and there the cattle grid sign comes in sight meaning—*slow down*.

Typical road with a grid

There is a roadhouse every few hundred kilometres, which is a dusty building with a gas station next to it and a basic grocery store. The buildings are both somewhat rough and neat at the same time. There are travellers working in them—largely the 'work and holiday visa' people from overseas.

A fresh wreck of an otherwise new-looking Toyota Prado is on its roof near the roadside, with all sorts of clobber and camping gear strewn around it. We stop and look for people. There are none. Something happened. Somebody must have given them a lift in emergency. To hospital maybe?

With continuous rain, we notice the Floodway signs[2] for the first time. All of a sudden the flood poles along the road start to make sense. Flash floods they call them. Sometimes we see an occasional stream of water flowing across the road, otherwise large steady pools. Meanwhile the rain gets even thicker and there is no end in sight. One day after another. We put the tent up in rain, we pack it up in rain again. We eat in rain and go to pee in rain.

Floods at the Western Australian coast

The car is full of moisture, the fan heating is on full speed, the windshields are fogged. I can hardly see anything ahead. It's pounding and the sky is dark grey. The water pools get bigger and longer—now a few hundred metres each. Some of them have quite a strong current. Our car isn't built for that, that's for sure. The longest pool so far had water level reaching just half-way up to the tyre top. It doesn't feel good. There are mighty 4WD's coming down from the other side—nothing of our hatchback sort that would give some comfort. The rain is unforgiving. The last water obstacle is right before the town of Carnarvon. It's longer and deeper. I am already thinking about what we'd do if the engine died right in the middle of it. Everybody is happy to get out of there and wouln't be quick to help some stuck losers. We have to push on. Once finally through, we decide to stay in a caravan because by now we're completely soaked. But the mattress inside the caravan didn't escape the rain either. It's all wet from a leak in the roof and so there's only one other bed left. It's sticky, warm and humid. In the morning, we jump over all the pools leading to the Reception. In the local information centre they tell us that the road south, the one we arrived yesterday, is now officially closed. The road north, the one we need to take is still open, but flooded with long water patches. They don't recommend that we go but it's up to us. Carnarvon is a small town and apart from banana plantations there is little to see. We're going.

15
From Sea to Mountains

We call our friend car mechanic in Perth. *How deep in water can we go with our small car?* It depends how high the engine air outlet is. About a foot should be all right. But there is one thing that can help, he says. Take a big rubbish bag and throw it over the front of the engine so that it hangs down and covers the registration plate. Close the bonnet over the bag and slowly go. It has to be a "constant and continuous drive with no stopping, so that water flows underneath the bag isolated from the engine". We go across, slowly, patiently. The mechanic was probably just having a lend of us while answering an idiotic question, but it seemed to work. Or it may have been just pure luck.

Finally, the rain becomes less intense. We have to stop and dry. Near Coral Bay, we stop next to a caravan. The people invite us in. Jim and Anne come from New Zealand but live in Brisbane. Their kids are living in their house while they're on the road. It's been two years now. They are retired and enjoy travel. It's a lifestyle thing. People even sell their houses and buy superbly equipped caravans.

The last water patch is slightly more daunting and looks like a creek. Then, as though by the wave of a magic wand, the rain stops at last. And although the heavy clouds remain, it's the first time in a week we can rest outside.

There are hundreds of strange-looking things to the left and right of the road that look like loads of something brown. Some of them small, some of them massive; they are everywhere. We're going to call them piles until we find out what they are.

North West Cape Peninsula is a promontory separated from the rest of Australia by Exmouth Gulf. The road is endless. Thanks to the local coral reef called Ningaloo Marine Park, it's a place for divers from all over Western Australia. The reef is not large, only about 280 kilometres, but it's unusually close to the shore, a miniature answer to the Great Barrier Reef in Queensland. It's an isolated place with one road wrapped around it—one that ends somewhere past the Cape Range National Park. Ideal for snorkelling, and when the season strikes from March to June, whale sharks, the largest living sea fish, arrive here and you can swim and dive with them. If you want.

In just about the middle of the peninsula, there is an interesting but closed area. Here be dragons—so to speak. An American Naval Communication Station is officially on the map not far from Exmouth, but apparently the whole place is a military playground nobody seems to know much about. It's a navy surveillance complex monitoring traffic in both the Indian and Pacific Oceans officially. Leaked information about its nuclear applications was all but shushed some time ago. It's situated ideally—on a landmass separated by both sea and ocean, on a hill, and it's got a lot of space to play with if needed where nobody will ever go. There are some narrow paths with *No Entry* signs from the main road.

Because of the small human population on the peninsula, there is a thriving animal habitat. Kangaroos roam freely, some of them quite large and so being cautious may pay off. An emu family is crossing the road and silhouettes of a few large wind turbines start to peak on the horizon.

Emu crossing the road near Exmouth

Cape Range National Park is just around the corner, not far after Exmouth[3]. We go uphill, towards Vlaming Head—a large lighthouse with a nice lookout. We are enjoying the slightly improved weather in the local caravan park, and kill time trying to fish on a small jetty. About a two-hour drive remains to reach the national park from the town. The jetty is rather fragile and something big is slowly swimming in the water near it. The hefty dose of rain and strong gusts of wind at night seem to go along with the weather forecast, still it improves the next day. Before long there is sun and we can stop at Yardie Creek[4]—a place to be, if one has a kayak or a canoe.

Canoeing in Yardie Creek, WA

We don't have one, but never mind because we can admire wallabies from very close when strolling up the rocky gully upstream. They live here in perfect symbiosis with the surrounding brownish walls. They are the same colour and so are not easily spotted. Their jumping skill on the rocky surface is something to think about. Another traveller tells us the brown piles all around us are actually giant termite mounds.

The next stretch after leaving Exmouth will be long. We're driving inland to the local highlands. Tom Price is about 550 kilometres away inland. Cars are rather rare in these parts, and what's even more amazing is the calmness when stepping outside somewhere on the long stretch of road, silence that blocks ears, so quiet it is. Three hundred and sixty degrees of nothing. Every now and then a cow or a kangaroo crosses the road. The mild coastal air is becoming crisp, as if it were mountains. Hill tops start popping up near Paraburdoo, but they are different—reddish in colour. We are higher and higher above the sea level. We need to push eighty more kilometres but it's getting dark and there is virtually nothing now between a small township of Tom Price. Only shrubs and rocks along the way, from which every moment a kangaroo might jump out and wreck the car. Kangaroos are not a problem in daylight. They are fast and vanish quickly from sight. They are confident creatures. They often stop and watch the car getting closer, only to jump out of the way at the very last moment. Kangaroos don't have excellent sight, but knowing they are quick, they have bad anticipation of speed—especially at night when the head lights even attract them as something curious. "Hey what's that light there around the bush? Must be early sunrise! Let's check it out fellas!"

An average adult roo might easily weight eighty kilos—and so the impact on the car is significant. We monitor the roadside closely for any animal shapes. It's quite a strain on the eyes, especially after 500 kilometres or so. There are roaming cows too, but they are more intelligent and don't tempt fate so much. Plus they are slower. There is one other thing that plays against kangaroos. Unlike cats and other predators, their eyes don't reflect light and don't glow which means they don't wear yellow vests. These are our ponderings in the middle of a perfect pitch-dark night. And we don't know where we're staying tonight. The local backpackers' should be a perfect choice in preparation for the local unique colourful mountains.

16
Iron Prince of Pilbara: Tom Price

In 1952, a special guest paid a visit to the would-be town called Tom Price. Lang Hancock, an Australian billionaire and natural resource magnate, touched down in his private jet. He stepped out, and with the eye of an insider, he started to wonder about the beauty of the surrounding landscape. He bent down and scooped up a bit of the dirt that was everywhere around him, and caressed it gently. He let it fall through his fingers: "There."

What he held in his hands was top-quality iron ore. He was imagining giant trucks crisscrossing the local endless horizons, kilometre-long trains, mammoth-sized ships and industrial harbours that would take all that to the world markets.

"Yeah," he muttered again, walking back to his plane while shaking off the dust off his hands: "Let's get out of here."

In those times the industry was under a government embargo because it wasn't known if there was enough of iron ore to justify exports.

But Hancock knew. He was not hallucinating. His visions started to materialise in 1961 when the embargo was lifted and a new empire was born. From that time, Tom Price—the highest situated town in Western Australia at 747 metres above the sea—has been dubbed the Iron Crown of Pilbara. What used to be Hamersley Ranges is today officially called by its traditional name, Karijini, and it became a national park. Well, part of it anyway. Why would they call the town Tom Price? Thomas Moore Price was a vice-president of Kaiser Steel, which would make him—a client. "Oh, gentlemen, what a nice present to call the town after me! I promise I'll buy more!" Anyway, this guy was popular and even though hands changed, the empire still exists—conveniently tucked away from the curious eyes of most because not many people come to this place. This, without exaggeration, is one of the most remarkable places in Australia.

It is here that the other face of Australia begins. One that 500 million years ago used to be seabed and it left unique scars[5].

Giant cracks of Karijini, WA

Millions of years of elements—water, fire, wind—have created spectacular landscapes. Layer after layer of different rock sediments make up walls that go deep and deeper into the earth and narrow down into a red labyrinth of colourful hellish-like gullies.

We've been driving on that hard red dirt for about thirty kilometres and wonder if the road is going to be as bad all along. We are on Banjima Drive[6]—the approximately 100-kilometre and most interesting stretch that goes through the heart of the park. It's known as unsealed or corrugated road and is made of stones of different sizes and grades, and also an endless number of parallel ridges created by water, only a few inches apart, which at times disappear completely, or intensify to such a degree that the steering wheel starts to shake uncontrollably until the truly non-4WD Corolla slows down to about ten to twenty kilometres per hour. To see the most interesting places, we need to conquer about eighty kilometres on this road. It is worth it.

Banjima Drive: the road to gorges

17
The Nanny

In Australia, things simply work. There are signs everywhere: warnings, tags, announcements, notifications, leaflets. If a road is being fixed, it's clearly marked, signposted, and fenced. Two guys are sweating their arses off in a ditch, while four others (at least) are standing nearby holding stop signs in each direction like human sculptures all day long so everybody knows there is roadwork in progress. They are called lollipop ladies. Here is a special sign you can't do this, there is another sign you're not allowed to do that, here are other warnings that something else might happen to you if you don't comply. You see them everywhere. Often there are about twenty no-no's on one big board listing "can't do" stuff. What a considerate mindful country. It would be easier and less costly for material to actually make signs with "can do" items. Common sense used to take care of most of these things. If I slip on a bloody banana and break my leg, I can only put it down to my own carelessness. I should have looked better, because it was right there in front of me! The modern approach is more of a blame game: people are immediately invited to ask whose pavement and whose banana it was.

Some years ago a surfer got a massive payout from a council for breaking his neck on the beach because he was swimming in an area marked safe. That part of the beach was the council's domain, with life saver volunteers in place. He didn't know that swimming comes with risk even between the flags. Another signpost needed, or just more common sense?

Once, I wanted to buy a ninety-five per cent spirit alcohol for a health recipe, and I had to prove to the booze shop owner that I was not a nutter who was going to drink it straight. Because an eighteen-year old died some years earlier after drinking an unthinned shot. He might lose his liquor licence. There was talk about banning the stuff altogether. Again, more rules and pointing fingers, or more individual responsibility and common sense? The modern system of governance increasingly prefers to do the thinking part for you perhaps to make up for your dwindling self-preservation instincts. It comes with a tag called 'for your own safety'. The resulting *nanny state* tries to prevent everything before it happens and it sneaks its way into the Australian mentality that is not used and supposed to openly criticise authority. This comes in different shapes and degrees in different Australian states and has its historical roots.

If the state decideds that something is necessary for the common good, the rules and regulations take over and may sometimes have the tendency to overwrite common sense. They are double-edged swords. They can work well in some instances but be counterproductive and infringing in others especially whencarried out to extremes. They are hardly ever retracted and often become a new accepted norm that is no longer supposed to be questioned.

Sound gun regulations can save lives by keeping dangerous weapons out of the hands of unstable individuals. In 1996, a madman killed 36 people in what's known as the Port Arthur massacre. It was a shocking tragedy. That's why I can't legally buy a slingshot in most Australian states today. "Everybody raise your hands, it's a robbery!" shouts a masked SLINGSHOT man to terrified staff at a typical Australian bank branch.

Fluoride helps prevent tooth decay. Used in toothpaste, it can be good for your teeth. So why don't we exaggerate a scheme to dump millions of tonnes of industrial waste called fluoride—an abundant by-product of phosphate production—into drinking water and conveniently relieve the multi-billion dollar industry of what would otherwise be a very expensive waste disposal problem.

"Mum, are there teeth in my stomach?"

Vaccines saved millions of lives worldwide. Whooping cough, tetanus, diphtheria, poliovirus, measles, hepatitis B, you name it, diseases that no longer exist because a regulated and thoroughly tested treatment has been proven to provide immunity and stop transmission or eradicate the pathogen altogether. Imagine, however, a situation where a newly developed, poorly tested and only conditionally approved drug with zero safety data which neither provides immunity nor stops transmission, for a disease that has 99.97 per cent survival rate, is required to be injected by the entire population or else you will be fired fom your job. Unelected health bureaucrats would then start spreading panic in all the mainstream media and lock you down in your homes until they get their way.

"By self-inflicting a heavy blow to your head with a one-kilogram steel club hammer, you will be better prepared to receive a meteorite should it ever land on your person in the future".

Nah! That could never happen in Australia!

Try to go to any farmer and buy some raw milk because you just happened to be in the countryside somewhere and you're thirsty. Good luck with that. Selling raw milk products is illegal in Australia, with heavy fines. No help if you are educated and fully aware of the dangers and would always boil it first. Hey, but you can still buy a cow and get your own milk.

The consumers are treated as children. There are no grown-ups any more. Rules and regulations can keep people from plunging into the abyss if the threat of a hefty fine keeps them from entering a restricted area. Australia's mountains may not look it, but they are some of the most treacherous in the world. So the rules about entering some places and not others are well justified.

On the other hand, if I lack the slightest elementary instinct for self-preservation and impulsively decide to take a picture on a rapidly descending cliff edge behind a well-marked fence around a beautiful lookout point, no warning sign or regulation will ever save me. One day I may become a popular rock imprint in a museum called 'A Backpacker with a Selfie Stick'.

You might as well close all the spectacular places to the public, because one day someone might fall in. And it's not a joke. It's happening.

Yesterday a tourist fell into one of the local gorges. The rescue team came from Newman, about 250 kilometres away, and it took them all day to pull the poor soul out of the narrow crevasse. It's an expensive operation. There are medics and professionals, equipment, gear, a helicopter, hundreds of man-hours, high risk to someone else's life, in other words, precious resources used for something that could have been avoided.

In the current Australian legal system, if someone is negligent and causes someone else harm, there are legal avenues and levers to sue. *Duty of care* is a legal term that describes the obligation of any person or organisation to protect others from foreseeable harm. If they don't, and it can be proved beyond reasonable doubt, there are likely to be consequences and financial implications.

In this kind of environment, it is much easier for national parks to use safety as an excuse to close tracks altogether. They simply become liabilities, with little benefit to them and a huge obligation to maintain them. They play it safe. A bit unfortunate for a country with such enormous potential, you might say. Safety concerns are the second most common reason, after political correctness, why many interesting places have disappeared from the maps and official guides in recent years, or have been closed to the public. The most notable examples are the Uluru climb in the Northern Territory, closed in 2019, Mount Warning in NSW, closed in 2022, or large parts of Grampians in Victoria, closed to walking, climbing and camping in 2023 under threat of draconian, ridiculous fines.

The people who arrive in Karijini in Western Australia are still more of inquisitive explorers, rather than the city comfort seekers in droves. If bitumen roads through the park are built one day and the mainstream tourism hits the place, nobody knows how things will play out. Would the tracks be marked with *No Entry* or *Access with Guides Only* signs? Would Karijini become the second Uluru in a perfect 'look but don't touch' reality?

The Nanny wants to keep everybody safe to minimise the risks or eliminate them altogether. Since times immemorial though, life has always been inseparable from risk. The rules are good when they underline—not overwrite—common sense. They can never replace sound individual judgement.

18
Walking On Ore: Karijini National Park

Karijini National Park was once known as Hamersley Ranges after Edward Hamersley—a rich early settler who made money on the colonial politics of land distribution. The place got back its traditional name only towards the end of the twentieth century.

Karijini boasts one of the largest deposits of iron ore in the world and the local hills are literally red in colour. It wouldn't be much of an overstatement to say you're actually walking on iron ore. When looking at the landscape from above, you can't help but thinking that somebody from somewhere up the celestial ladder has cut the earth with a giant knife. There are deep ravines and gorges, and you can look into some of them and actually walk them down too. First, however, you need to get to them by a rather bumpy road.

Inside one of the gorges of Karijini, WA

There are two roads to Karijini from the west—one from Tom Price and the second one from Paraburdoo. Both of them will merge into Karijini Drive[7], from which we need to turn to the bumpy Banjima Drive. After thirty kilometres or so we're finally at the gorges: Hancock Gorge, Joffre Gorge, Weano Gorge, Red Gorge, Wittenoom Gorge, and Knox Gorge[8]. Sometimes it's a walk along steep walls, sometimes through narrow crevasses: local maps and guides rate them into several difficulty levels. The more interesting are fours, fives and sixes.

There is water at the bottom, either a fast-running stream or larger pools good enough for liloing—riding on inflatable mattresses. Cockatoos fly and rest inside the walls and they are fairly close sometimes. Handrail Pool is at the bottom of a chained path leading to a rocky enclosure. Weano Gorge is a starting point to get there.

Descending a gorge

Knox Gorge however is probably the best. Once we get down, the track is forking into two paths. The one to the right is a beautiful river surrounded by colourful rocks on both sides—a photographer's paradise. The shorter one on the left leads to a place where a huge boulder is stuck between opposing walls.

We can get on top of it but the stream underneath disappears suddenly and it is not clear how far and how deep. We are at the bottom of a narrow crevice balancing over a gushing stream of water.

Boulder in Knox Gorge

Joffre Falls on the way back is a great swimming place. That's reserved for the next day though. We sleep in the Savannah campground.

The local aboriginal community is in charge of it. It's nice, clean, there is deafening silence at night and there is a bush shower—a very inventive one. Warm water from a large tank on the roof is tapped into a pouch with a nozzle, raised up on a rope; and we have two minutes of perfect water refresher.

The tourism industry is microscopic compared to the stakes in the mining industry juggernaut. The area is mainly used by primary industries that not so gently scar the local landscape in the name of economic growth.

The heavy weights aren't visible at first. The whole national park is cut in half by a narrow corridor, a train line which goes along about a 300-kilometre railway track from the giant open mine pit at the foot of Mount Bruce to an industrial harbour in Dampier.

Bush shower, Karijini, WA

The track is formally outside the national park boundaries and is used by extremely long trains. It's equipped with sensors so that somebody at a desk in a remote city office can monitor whether they're fit for millions of tonnes of iron ore rolling on them every day. To see the trains, though, in their full splendour, we need to walk up the second highest peak of Western Australia. Therefore, the whole next day is reserved for Mount Bruce.

Railway track near Mount Bruce / Punurrunha, WA

The first part of the nine-kilometre trek offers breath-taking views—a huge theatre stage on which two slow-moving two-kilometre long snake-like trains are passing each other—each of them having two large engines—in opposite directions. The empty train will be passing the full one for a good hour. We're counting the number of cars, stopping at 230 or so. The mine itself is still out of sight from this angle. We're sweating before getting to the top but the reward is great. Over two hundred carriages full of iron ore, up to 100 tonnes of it each. That's enough to make fifteen thousand cars, they say. Two-hundred tonne large capacity trucks that move forth and back look like small brown beetles. Where there is a giant hole in the ground today was once a mountain similar to the one we're standing on.

While the empty "snake" is ready to be loaded by the "beetles", the full one is already on its way to the Dampier shipping harbour—the largest of its kind in Australia. It had to be specially deepened for the fully loaded ships that would take fifty million tonnes of iron ore out to sea each year.

View from Mount Bruce / Punurrunha[9], 1,234 m ASL

Other peaks are visible from Mount Bruce: Mount Vigors, Mount King, Mount Frederick. We're a bit confused as to the name of the highest peak in Western Australia. Some said it was Mount Nameless / Jarndunmunha at 1,128 metres above the sea, accessible from Tom Price. But we're higher at 1,234 metres. Something's not adding up. Are we perhaps on the highest peak? No. Apparently Mount Nameless is the highest mountain accessible by car. Mount Bruce / Punurrunha is said to be second and the champion is Mount Meharry / Wirlbiwirlbi at 1,245 metres. The road to it goes through private land.

That night in the Dales Camping Area, we see dingoes for the first time. They wake us up in the middle of the night when they scavenge through the rubbish bins. The torch beam scares them off and they quickly disappear into the darkness.

Nothing can beat Karijini from now on. At least that's what we think the next day, when it's time to leave.

19
Salt, Tibet And the Prophecy of Port Hedland

Karijini Drive—the only bitumen road across the national park—takes us away to the east and then north again to Port Hedland. It's true the landscape is nothing like the usual boring stuff we saw all around before coming here. The area is rocky, hilly and interesting. Auski Roadhouse is another service station in the middle of nowhere. Port Hedland is a dual-town, and no, it's not a spelling mistake. We stop at South Hedland, the more populated part. The Port is exactly what is says: the port. There is another giant train arriving—this time full of salt. It's produced here by solar evaporation and the few facilities make eight million tonnes or so of it, in excellent quality for export, through the same port used for the iron ore.

A bunch of local Aboriginal guys are drinking wine from goon bags in a shady part of the park, a huge rusty industrial facility in their backdrop. It's very hot, the town is empty and there is nothing else to do.

Industrial backdrop in Port Hedland

Two people in the local camp are about to make our day. One of them is in the course of crossing Australia on a pushbike, the other one is a prophet.

"I've come from Melbourne, heading for Melbourne," says the former.

Brian is the first of the army of cyclists we meet crossing the continent. He's been on the road for two years now. His mission is to help children of Tibet. When he was in Tibet, he happened to snoop in some unofficial places and he stumbled across a guy on the local market who handed him a scrap of paper with "Help children of Tibet" on it.

"You know," he explains with some irritation in his voice, "in Tibet, you can't go wherever you want to, they'll give you a guide who is going to be Chinese—guaranteed! They will show you what the government wants you to see. Lots of Tibetan children live in India in terrible conditions with little prospect of a future." Brian is a volunteer of an Adelaide-based organisation trying to financially help them."

He has modified his bike for long-distance rides. He pulls a bob trailer behind him with necessary minimum of spare parts and tools. The less, the better. A miniature tent that just fits a miniature stove. Miniature everything.

"If you want to go around Australia on a bike, you need to read books by those who've done it before like Paul Elwood. The biggest problem is water. It weighs and seems heavier every new kilometre. And even though you know the water sources on the way, at some places there is no water at all, meaning, you need to carry sixteen litres of it sometimes." That's not a very comfy proposition. There is a spot in the Kimberleys with water only because a guy made a rest place on his private land there. They say his son got killed in a car accident and he wanted to remember him that way.

"And what are you doing here?" we ask a woman standing next to him. "I am touring around Australia. My engine blew up." I am waiting for a new one I ordered. I went three thousand kilometres and I didn't check the oil," she says calmly. "Yeah, check your oil if you can. Don't end up like me. Each morning before setting out. It costs me more than the whole car".

The stretch from Port Hedland to Broome is 600 kilometres through a long edge of a desert with one stop only approximately in the middle—the Sandfire Roadhouse[10]. The desert on that side doesn't actually look like a desert at all: it's more of a wasteland with combination of scrub and sand on both sides. You can even see cows at the side of the road sometimes.

We plan to make it in one day and are ready: supplies, water, checking tyres, petrol. We're already driving when we remember the words from yesterday. The engine oil. On opening the hood, I can't believe my eyes. The engine is splattered with grease. There is a massive leak through a broken seal. Luckily, we're not far from the town and quickly turn for the nearest service station. The repair is nothing compared to what would have happened if we discovered it later in the day. That would be end. The woman was sent by heaven.

20
Great Sandy Desert

The Sandfire Roadhouse, in the middle of the Great Sandy Desert, where we sleep tonight, in between Port Hedland and Broome, is lush greenery that looks more like a zoo than desert. Thousands of small insects in the shower are prepared to ambush anyone who is foolhardy enough to put the light on. A large green frog sits glued to the window wall next to the toilet seat.

Australia is said to have made three historically significant mistakes: the first was the stolen generation, the second one was sending soldiers into the WWI and the third was the cane toad—the so called *Bufo Marinus*. They introduced it as a "natural" protection of sugar cane against pests. In short, it was to eat anything that eats the sugar cane. And it did. Except the toad took the initiative to a different level. It downed literally everything it could get its tongue on, alive or dead (it made little difference), and that created a mishmash in its stomach so toxic that every animal further up the feeding chain was faced with agonising death by poisoning. Between 1935 and 1980, the toad infested the whole north-east of the country, and if it weren't for the desert, it would be here too. It's clear this one is a harmless frog.

Harmless frog at Sandfire Roadhouse's showers, WA

We nicely put the tent up under a tall tree. The sky is perfectly clear in the morning but the tent is wet, as though it had rained heavily overnight.

"That's not rain, that's a hundred per cent humidity," says somebody from the neighbouring tent on the left.

"The tree has peed on you during the night."

A group of young girls came in an old car like ours and they now sit and sip their morning coffees next to the tent on the right.

"Condensation."

They've just got up while we're almost ready to go. This will turn against them that very evening. The sun dries the tent within minutes. We set out to finish the remaining 300 kilometres or so of the unbelievably straight *desert* road. All we can see is shrubs and flat land. Hours of it on both sides. This is what one and the only road from the south to the town of Broome looks like.

Many expeditions have scoured this part of the coast since the eighteenth century, and they started to systematically record their findings about the new mysterious continent in the south seas. The sources of the time were in no mood to suggest that one day (or ever) any European settler would feel like setting foot on something so inhospitable, let alone trying to settle or colonise it. Still back in 1803 the French explorer Commodore Nicholas Baudin and later Louis de Freycinet reported that:

The coast from the moment we saw it exhibited nothing but a picture of desolation; no rivulet consoled the eye, no tree attracted it; no mountain gave variety to the landscape, no dwelling enlivened it. Everywhere reigned sterility and death.[11]

So much for the French.

The British colonial interests only bothered to take the west coast more seriously later and that mainly because of prospecting new pastoral land, and also because of excess of rotting boats full of prisoners on the Thames.

On arrival at the intersection to Broome, we know for sure we're in the tropics. One stop at a petrol station and we're sweating like pigs. The absence of the aircon is not the problem, but you need to be on the move. If you stop, you feel it. Not long after we're in Broome, a town they don't write much about these days. For somebody who has no clue about what happened here in the past, the town might look nothing much like a jewel. Tourism is the industry of the day and the beaches and caravan parks are chock-a-block. Night-life in the centre looks busy. There are backpackers, tourists, locals. An aboriginal woman is trying to pour boxed wine into a two litre plastic bottle. She is sitting on the ground and her hands are shaking so much that most of it ends up on the pavement. Larger four-litre *goon* is not on sale here. Unostentatious Broome has written history twice, with the first event being tightly connected to the second. From about the middle of the nineteenth century, mother-of-pearl was collected here (eighty per cent of the whole world's production at one stage) and then—although not many are keen to let it on and write about it—it staged one of the most blood-soaked chapters of the British colonisation of Australia.

21
Indigenous Versus Conventional: Take II

When the famous buccaneer William Dampier with his bunch of mates were circling the west coast of Australia in 1688 and circumstances forced him to take a maintenance break, he recorded in his diary while his crew was fixing his Cygnet:

The inhabitants of this country are the miserablest people in the world. The Hottentots, though a nasty people, yet for wealth are gentlemen to these; who have no houses and skin garments, sheep, poultry, and fruits of the earth, ostrich eggs and so on, as the Hottentots have. And setting aside their human shape, they differ but little from brutes. They are tall, straight-bodied, and thin with small, long limbs. They have great heads, round foreheads, and great brows. Their eyelids are always half-closed, to keep the flies out of their eyes, they being so troublesome here, that no fanning will keep them from coming to one's face ... so that from their infancy being thus annoyed with these insects, they do never open their eyes as other people: and therefore they cannot see far, unless they hold up their heads, as if they were looking at somewhat over them.[12]

The British did treat them as such. At that time until the beginning of the twentieth century, the papers were full of scientific essays about the genetic supremacy of the white race. The natives were regarded as bludgers and lazy-bones, who quickly and willingly adopted from the civilisation all the "good stuff", such as cigarettes or alcohol, but the "bad stuff", like work, was not their thing. To be more precise, work didn't apply to them at all, because material gain had no place in their culture. They interpreted life by spiritualism based on stories about animals, trees, caves, and so on and lived only on what they needed, mainly bush tucker.

For the new landlords, this counted as a clear evidence that what they have to suffer on their newly acquired lands were a bunch of idling loafers: They were at least going to work in stables and collect the pretty white little balls that grow in the sea. And categorically no money. They'd only spend it on booze!

Already, around 1880, the business went quite well. The pretty white little balls in the sea were aplenty, and before the natives gathered them up around the shores of Broome, the colony started to indulge in a new and lucrative trade—mother-of-pearl. Now they had to go deeper into the sea. Those who better mastered that skill, came out on top. Or to put it more bluntly—whoever had people who would do it for him—was coming out on top.

What happened to Aboriginal people in Broome is a very good representation of what was happening to them all around the country. The Aborigines could hardly defend themselves. Even if somebody cared, in those times a piece of news took months to even get out of the country. This was a totally isolated place, a remote outpost of the empire, that only a relatively few had access to. The colonies were not quick to let out anything that would compromise the interests of the monarchy. The world at that time had enough other problems.

The curiosity and interest of natives in their new visitors didn't last long. The first contacts were friendly, but when everybody went about their usual business, the old and new worlds proved to be incompatible. After a short indifference, the relations quickly deteriorated and then the colonisers took over and completely annihilated everything around them. The aboriginal defence was based on loud exclamations as a proof they were not afraid of the enemy. Their visible parades in the first encounters only made it easier for the other side to take better aim of their targets. They were badly outnumbered, and without firearms.

When the colonial might was handing out the land, its inhabitants became property of the new masters. Later, even *half casts*—how those of mixed parentage were called—could be dragged into forced education any time. Between 1900 and 1970, there were whole stolen generations of children who had been taken from their homes and placed in institutions. About fifty thousand or so. There were times when the British colonies differed from the American slavery system only in the fact that the British didn't have to import their slaves.

Farmers around Broome quickly understood that cattle was not going to make them rich. Looking after herds was hard strenuous work, the Aborigines were still spearing their cows, making the pastoralists even more furious, and the Kimberley Range was too hard a barrier to cross. So when the news of a new commodity broke out, all kinds of greedy rabble were arriving: from ex-cons through to unfulfilled bureaucrats sick of cities, to miners and gold diggers who couldn't sustain families. Having thirty or forty Aborigines working on boats for a few days could equal an average yearly income for next to no effort.

"You were not at the bottom!", yells the master. "Next time you go down, you present a bedrock! And shut up! No talking!" If one of them tried to reach for the boat, they were hit across their fingers. It wasn't rare even for a pregnant women to be forced to dive.

And we're talking going deeper and deeper. Bleeding nose was no excuse, some of them were getting strange pain in their arms, others lost consciousness or died unexpectedly. They didn't know about the bends or the decompression disease in those times. The dead stayed in the sea or were buried in the sand, right above the high tide mark. There were some who swam away, trying to escape. The master knew they didn't stand a chance.

The brutality had gone on to such a degree that in 1873 the government ruled no more women and children would be employed on the boats. The labour was hiding, of course, and so "recruitment" expeditions were organised. The market for blacks was thriving because no white man could be talked into working in such outrageous conditions. For any money. The slaves were taken off by force or voluntarily handed over and sold for a bit of food or drink by their own. Capturing or shooting an *Abo* had a tariff price. Five pounds. If they tried to resist, they were brutally punished. Often they were seized with "witnesses"—typically their women, who were chained to boab trees and repeatedly raped in front of their men. If a white settler lost his life during those expeditions by hand of any of the natives, a popular punishment was to tie the guilty one by his neck on a noose and drag him behind a horse through needle-sharp spinifex.

I don't want the town to be named after me, protested the governor of Western Australia, Sir Frederick Napier Broome. *It's going to be a ghost town soon*, he complained. Too late. The name had already been set in the printers. And it didn't become a ghost town either. The pearl industry grew and modernised. From 1880, special equipment was necessary to go even deeper and the local Aborigines were no longer in demand.

After about two decades of their intensive ruthless exploitation, hundreds of new settlers made fortunes. Nothing was left for the natives. Quite the contrary: with ruined health, alcohol addiction, and newly imported diseases, they were cast aside for a slow, agonising death.

And that's how Broome was born. A town with an amazing but unbelievably brutal past, so typical throughout the country. Nobody seems to be too quick to acknowledge that this was the very base of the newly creating state.

22
Tourist Broome

We pay for the last available spot at the Mango Camping Area. The three girls we met at the Sandfire Roadhouse didn't make it on time. There is only one road from Broome after all, and we meet the same travellers.

Broome has relatively wide streets with palm and banana trees alongside. The local jetty, hundreds of metres long, sticks out into the sea and is impressive. Fishermen are all around it.

A mighty boab tree near Broome, WA

In 1912—in the same year the Titanic sank—a steamboat arrived here from Perth, with twelve Royal Navy divers on board. They arrived because one year earlier a law had been introduced preventing the pearl boat owners hiring non-white crews. We're in the middle of the White Australia policy—the times of the British cultural hegemony. At that time about half of Broome was in Asian hands. Large Chinese and Japanese quarters powered most of the town's economy and the government lost its cool. The pearling industry here was mainly controlled by the Japanese. They stood out with their incredible diligence, discipline and hard work, and managed to have the upper hand, not only in the pearl business but also a significant influence on the social life of the town. They built a hospital of their own and the Japanese doctor was held in higher regard than the local one. There is an interesting theory about why there were so many Japanese.

A bunch of frustrated guys from Wakayama province is said to have walked through Melbourne during the famous Melbourne Cup in 1890. For a good few years they had been struggling to establish a decent living in Australia. The Melbourne Cup is sort of a national holiday. The few minutes of the horse race can bring the whole country to a halt as everybody checks their favourites. The boys checked theirs too and it was their lucky day. They'd won 22,500 pounds, which at an average yearly wage of about 100 pounds was a mind-bending sum. What are we going to do with it now, they thought? And so they invested in a fleet of boats in Broome—a town somewhere in the north-east of the country where rumours were going around of quick easy riches made out of the sea, but nobody wanted to say a thing. Wakayama had since been full of stories of easy pickings in Western Australia. Thousands followed in the next few years. Their advanced organisational skills, tenacity and their will to work for less than the locals gave them a huge lead.

And that's also why the Crown was going out of its way to prove once and for all it could do without the Asian mobs. And so the specially trained divers were able to dive for pearls with the same efficiency and vigour as the Asians.

The boys, however, were different kind of professionals—mainly helping in bridge construction or salvaging shipwrecks. They mostly worked in the murky waters of England and they were deployed in one-off operations. While having to stick to strict standards back at home, where they already knew much about the health implications of diving, their new employers in Australia took the divers' charts for less than bullshit. That was only hampering higher productivity and they could otherwise employ an Asian for three times less money. With the exorbitant wage rates paid to them, and the extra hours of surfacing, they were coming across as nothing but lazy whingers. Within a year, though, one of them was dead and two others were permanently paralysed. It didn't work.

Nobody knows today how many non-white divers died. The Asians were treated as foreigners despite being born in Australia, and the Aborigines have been counted as Australians only since 1971.

Being at the Japanese Cemetery[13] in Broome and walking between the rows of graves is like breathing history. About a thousand gravestones are silent witness to times gone by. The names engraved in their language are largely of people who died very young—killed by pressure-inflicted injuries and other diseases the medicine of the time knew little about.

Japanese Cemetery in Broome, WA: Katsujiro Maekawa, died at the age of 26.

Today the Japanese are arriving in the town in coaches and within their fourteen-day holiday span: already having seen the complete Australian east coast, including Sydney and Melbourne, they come to spend a few hours in Broome, before finally departing for Darwin for the final days of their trips.

They are now enjoying the town on which they had such a tremendous influence. They are so well-mannered that whenever their tourist guides inadvertently mention something about bombing this place by kamikazes during WWII, apologetic voices can be heard at the back of the coach, "sorry, sorry, sorry".

At one particular place in Broome, a tourist sign points to a spot where dinosaur traces are to be seen.

We are going there. The spot, however, is three metres in water it turns out, because of the high tide, and all we can see is an information board. There is an incredible eleven-metre difference between low and high tides in Broome. Moreover, the dinosaur footprints are just cast in concrete. The originals, apparently—120 million years old or so—were stolen in 1997 by a network of international thieves. They were to be one of the few clear pieces of evidence at the time of dinosaurs having lived in Australia.

But the sunset here is really enthralling. The light reflected from the sea is said to create an optical illusion of a staircase gently rising to the very fringe of the full moon.

The overcrowded camp's tent section is young and busy. The caravan section is more settled, comfortable and cosy. The blinking lights are giving away TV screens; there are refrigerators, living rooms, kitchen cupboards, steaks are being prepared on hundred-kilo barbecue sets. Just why those people have to tow half their households on holidays with them remains a mystery. They probably want to live here, if only for a few days. It must be the smooth long beach—the incredibly flat, vast, unmatched elsewhere—the beautiful unforgettable beach.

These thoughts are slowly drifting us away deeper and deeper into sleep after fourteens days, about three and a half thousand kilometres, and with about twelve thousand more to go.

III. Broome to Darwin

23
"That Funny Hotel": From Fitzroy to Halls

We check the engine oil this time. Willare Bridge Roadhouse is about two hours away from Broome. A signpost is showing distances to nearest places. The next one is Fitzroy Crossing, 230 kilometres away, then Darwin, 1709 kilometres. While still in Perth, about two weeks ago, a friend of ours happened to mention in a between the lines kind of way: "When you get to Fitzroy Crossing, don't be scared by the hotel." When we asked what he meant by that, he said with a bit of a malicious smile, "You will see."

Shortly before Fitzroy Crossing there is a left turn to Leopold Downs Road, a dirt road, which would go for about hundred bumpy kilometres and then turn into Gibb River Road. A well-known place called Tunnel Creek is not far from here on that road, and about thirty kilometres after that another called Windjana Gorge. Both are miniature national parks. Tunnel Creek is an entry point to an extensive tunnel system, good to be explored with a torch. It was here in 1897 when Jandamarra—a *terrorist* in today's official doublespeak but always a hero to the natives—was shot to death. He was one of the very few Aboriginal rebels who openly stood up against the increasingly expansive settlers and was too elusive to be caught by them in his natural environment. The British had to recruit one of his own to get him. Apparently the authorities had been so jubilant about this that they celebrated it by cutting his head off and sending it to London in a jar as a marketing souvenir. Fresh-water crocodiles might live there, which lends those places an even more eerie feel.

Distances from Willare Bridge Roadhouse, WA

After about five kilometres into the dirt road we stop at a flooded stretch that isn't looking any good. You either go ahead or turn around. There is no other way. Go or not to go? That is the question. Al old Ford Falcon soon arrives from the other direction and faces the same problem. An Anglo-German-Dutch squad of three backpackers. It turns out these large pools are quite frequent on this rough road and might pose too big a challenge for a conventional car like ours. Their Ford's clearance is substantially higher though, yet it has to work really hard. Too much of a risk. We join them at the campground in Fitzroy.

The large number of houses on metal poles around Fitzroy surprise us. Apparently, the reason for this is twofold. One, there are termites virtually everywhere and they would chew the house from its base up to the top in the matter of days. And second, there are floods almost every year. The town was founded at a crossroad, a source of drinking water and a refuge from floods.

A truly historic hotel with a large terrace is said to be the oldest accommodation facility in the Kimberleys, dating from 1897. A small local information centre is quiet.

"Fitzroy Crossing has two campgrounds: Tarunda before the river and Fitzroy River Lodge after the bridge. Both are *safe*, even the one before the river is fenced," says an employee of the centre with a motherly smile.

"Why shouldn't it be safe?" we ask.

"You know. Today is a payday. You'll see."

The first smaller Tarunda campground is actually like a car park with a high fence around it. Spots are available but it's time to make a little trip around the town. A thick smoke can be seen in the distance. Back-burning, a way to control the bush—it's better to burn it a little by little at the right time than do nothing and wait for a disaster. A regular thing. The trick is to burn the tops without damaging the tree roots. Now, in close proximity to the road, a blazing three-metre-high flame is ruthlessly lashing any dry grass that stands in its way. We are trying to get back to the main road somehow and over the bridge to the other camp, and we pass simple houses where locals live.

Back-burning

A pub called Crossing Inn appears right after, and there are about twenty Aboriginal locals lying on the ground in front of it. They're enjoying their payday. A bit of a binge. A few heads are turning slowly as we pass them by. We have to drive carefully so as not to run over some of them. They are stretched all over. A pheasant-like bird with an extremely long tail is making a strange dance across the road not far from them.

Harry is an English backpacker who arrived here with a Work and Holiday visa, a status many Western countries enjoy in Australia, and a good idea too because it saves loads of money. You're allowed to work full time and earn enough cash to travel afterwards. Not a dumb system for Australia either because what you earn will stay in the country and support its economy. Many regional areas suffer from staff shortages and backpackers fill the gaps. Limited time is the downside. Many travellers arrive as students, on a status that except of being a bit of a rip-off—most colleges for international student are not worth the money—makes it very hard for them to leave a chosen city for more than a few days at a time, and also limits weekly working hours. Not meeting certain school attendance requirements means an automatic *adios*. The only other real alternative for any hope of a longer expedition is permanent residency, and this is not easy to come by. It's a long and painful assessment process that can discourage even the most patient individuals. The scoring system requires you to get enough points to match the profession and skill list, something that changes constantly according to Australia's current market demand, to prove the person's education from home and from Australia if it is finished successfully; it assesses your age category, work experience, the appropriate level of English, health condition, partner relations, that you are of good character, and so on and so forth. That's when all sorts of vultures descend on your bony skeleton to assist you in your quest to fulfil all the requirements Education agents skimming hefty commissions directly from schools so it looks like they do it for you out of sheer love, solicitors charging non-trivial fees for putting the paperwork together, plus other substantial fees for medical examinations, professional bodies certifications, language preparation courses and testing, proving clean criminal records from overseas and Australia, verifying the de facto relationship if one has a partner, and finding all the other smaller bits of the M. C. Escher's *Salita e Discesa* thousand-part jigsaw puzzle masterpiece, before you can submit the complete picture. Besides, the whole system constantly changes with the mood of those who are currently at the political steering wheel.

Work and Holiday is easier.

Harry's working phase is now safely behind him and he can concentrate on travels. His first job started exactly five months ago in Darwin. The advertisement was looking for kitchen staff and the owner was to pick him up at an agreed spot. A funny-looking pair, husband and wife, arrived to pick Harry up in a worn-down 4WD wrapped in red dust from tyres to the roof. It had an antenna on the front hood that was so high its upper end was getting lost in the sky.

The bearded guy didn't say much and neither did his wife. Short hello and off they went. They went for an hour, two, three hours, and the people didn't drop a single word. When it got dark and they hit a serious dirt road for the first time, Harry went a little edgy. He didn't want to tease his boss by impertinent questions right at the start, so he only casually remarked that he had never driven that far in his entire life and he was dying to see it on a map. Boss calmly replied he didn't have one and they would soon be there anyway. And that was it. A five-hour conversation. Harry was peeling potatoes the following few months but had he disappeared, he wouldn't have been the first. Harry knew something I didn't.

24
Vanishing Tourists Business

Ivan Milat is probably one of the front-runners on the list of well-known psychopaths. It looks as though he made killing innocent backpackers into his pastime, but not everything was as clear as it seemed. They proved seven murders by him.

On the January 25, 1990, an English hitchhiker by the name of Paul Onions decided to thumb a ride from Sydney. The guy who stopped was fine for an hour or so, then he turned weird and threatened to tie him up. Onions saw the rope and gun and after some commotion somehow managed to get the better of him, only just escaping in an oncoming car. He reported the incident and soon left the country.

In 1992 and not far from the same place, the remains of two women were found, later identified as missing British tourists. Both of them had strange incision marks around their spines, as if having been paralysed before death. Both girls' flies were unzipped. One had four bullets in her head. There was a small makeshift fireplace nearby. However, both victims were in such an advanced decomposition that not much could be established. Police denied any serial killer suspicion and continued a detailed and painstakingly slow investigation, including analyses of all cases of disappearance in the last ten years. A psychologist was employed in an attempt to decipher a mental picture of the possible maniac.

In 1993, more victims—this time an Australian couple—were found. They had disappeared in 1989. They had similarly unzipped trousers and a similar wound on the spines. A fireplace was also present. Police carried out a detailed search of the surrounding forest. Three days later, the last victims were found—a German couple missing from 1991. Ballistic fingerprints matched the ones previously discovered. One of the victims was without a head. and it was later suspected that skulls were used as targets. Police were now conceding for the first time that a serial killer could be involved. In 1994, the case was heavily promoted in the media, but that led to no significant progress until Paul Onions came back to Australia as a witness. His claim of having escaped a certain violent individual was confirmed by a woman, the driver of the car, who took him to a police station. If Onions recognised Milat, a warrant could be issued for his arrest, and that's what happened. A search of his numerous properties later revealed many artefacts belonging to the victims, and it also yielded the notorious weapon.

The trial started in 1996, and after a short time Milat sacked his defence lawyer because he had advised him to plead guilty. During his time in court, he vehemently denied any participation in the crimes, and some facts were actually playing for him. Firstly, he was a non-smoker and didn't drink, but there were large numbers of cigarette butts and empty bottles. Some of the evidence suggested that his family could be complicit, and that there were many more victims. Milat's fired defending lawyer, John Marsden, was to reveal before his death that he strongly suspected Milat had been helped by his sister. Later in 2007, evidence was sent to Britain for DNA tests on some of the items because the technology had not been available at the time of crimes. They were, however, not enough to charge anybody else.

After a fifteen-week trial, Milat was sentenced to six years for assault on Paul Onions and seven consecutive life sentences: one for each victim. He is doing his time in Goulburn Jail—one of the toughest places in Australia, with maximum security and bleak white clinical walls. All of his appeals against the sentence were rejected. Whenever he was asked about his crimes, he swore his innocence. He even swallowed metal objects to attract attention, and in 2009 he is said to have cut his finger with a plastic knife and wanted the case to be sent to the highest court.

"I don't miss my family so much. I miss my cat," says Harry suddenly.

"I can't send him an email."

25
United We Fall

The small national park called Geiki Gorge lies not even twenty-six kilometres from the town of Fitzroy Crossing. An English explorer, Sir Archibald Geiki, prospected this area back in 1883 and he was the first white in this place. The walls of the local information centre show watermarks—that's how high the water level is during floods. The highest one is right under the roof. In the wet season, floods can easily raise the water level by ten metres and spread sixteen kilometres away. The town can be cut off from the rest of the world for up to a month.

Geiki Gorge is a beautiful riverbed surrounded by massive rock formations and walking along its sand banks can be hard. There are flies everywhere and it's incredibly hot. The watermarks can be seen on the rock walls and not far from them, right in the middle of the river, a fresh-water crocodile is enjoying a sunbath. He might be about fifty metres away and doesn't let anybody disturb him.

Geiki Gorge, WA: River, crocodile, and rock wall

We meet the English-Dutch-German trio of backpackers in Halls Creek again which to our eyes is a carbon copy of Fitzroy Crossing. It's a small transit town with a significant population of Aboriginal people.

The information centre offers discounts on plane tours of the nearby Bungle Bungle National Park, also known as Purnululu. Two is a company, three is a crowd. They require three people at least to make it happen and that's where the European "alliance and solidarity" manifests itself in its full glory: The German-Dutch fraction is all for the game but the Englishman is "not dying to see it". In a desperate act of last resort, they turn to the East, but we're not interested either. The "European Union Plane" is flying nowhere. Helicopter tours are also available from Warmun Roadhouse in Turkey Creek—one stop after this one—but it's like going from rain under the gutter. It's even more expensive because the chopper's rotors need more special care than the plane's wings. Purnululu is otherwise hard to access, with a conventional hatchback anyway.

A charming shop assistant in the local souvenir shop and information centre in one is sorry for us and asks where we come from.

"Gee, I would take you there with my car if I had a four-wheel." The approximately fifty-kilometre long stretch to the Bungles is a rough ride, and we would be trying to bite off more than we can chew.

"Here you are," and to each one of us he hands out a photobook of the Bungle Bungles with super thick expensively coloured pages. "Complimentary, really," he says with a grin. "Really".

We're looking at one another. "Thank you."

"At least you're going to have nice pictures," he adds.

"That's very kind of you," we say, slightly embarrassed.

"Help yourselves to the pins or other souvenirs, anything for free, really."

We exchange even more baffled looks. This guy either wants to be fired or is pulling our leg.

Small section of the China Wall[14] near Halls Creek, WA

Halls Creek has an interesting natural phenomenon called China Wall—a long rock formation similar to a fence that goes for kilometres and disappears somewhere in the harsh, hilly and barren outback. The road seems like going through a private land, because after a few kilometres of gravel road there is a gate with a sign: *Shut this gate. Thanks.*

Not far from here, only some 150 kilometres or so, is the infamous Wolfe Creek Crater used for some TV creations to further reinforce the well preserved reputation of Australia as a bloody dangerous place.

We are parting with our three co-travellers in Turkey Creek Station, never to see them again. But we'll meet Harry just in a few months' time—this time in a few hundred thousand crowd at the Jazz Festival in the Sydney Domain. Australia is small.

26
Of Crocodiles and Men: Take I

From the last actual crossroad—some 830 kilometres from here—we're arriving in Wyndham, the Kimberley's northernmost town and a place that at first glance looks like the last outpost of nowhere. The town was discovered by white settlers around 1819 and they described it in such an awful way that for the next sixty years almost nobody else arrived.

On seeing the endless stretches of dry sea shore with sparkling and glittering salt all around, uninitiated travellers might be excused thinking, nothing could be more boring. But they would be wrong. In fact there are four incredible things you can't see anywhere else.

"Big crocodile" in Wyndham, WA

Australians like it big. A large crocodile is guarding the entry to the town after the first right turn. It can't be missed. It's eighteen metres long and is made of concrete. A perfect computer-designed crocodile[15]. Even the long truck parked next is much smaller. Secondly, the Big Aboriginal family[16] sculptures are not far from here. Another one of the big landmarks that decorate small, less significant Australian towns, dying to be known for something. There will be many more of them coming.

Big Aboriginal family sculptures in Wyndham, WA

Third is the Five River Lookout, which—as the name suggests—a view of five rivers. If you still have enough juice in you in this scorcher, the view will take the rest of your breath away.

Number four is a crocodile farm. That's where we're going now because one of the travellers we had met before knew the owner. The farm is almost at the end of the town road.

The oldest croc in service is retired and had he been a pup, he would wag his tail on hearing Bismark. Because that's his name. As the plaque near him puts it, he is seventy but feels forty. He loves life as long as there is anything to eat. And he eats everything. The scar on his back was given to him by one of his chums. So much for Bismark. His friend Oombi, in the next cell, is doing time here. In the Aboriginal town of Oombulgurri, he ate twenty-five local dogs—one of them directly from the leash. He was just about to put local children on his menu when he was captured and transported here, to his new asylum, surrounded by a harem of five females. He enjoyed them for a year or so, then got hopelessly bored. Sex wasn't his thing anymore.

We are slowly starting to understand what kind of habitat this northern Australia is surrounded by. Crocs are common in all rivers here and can swim hundreds of kilometres inland, especially during floods.

The crocodile is not an overly intelligent being. As a reptile—it's reminiscent of the ostrich in the bird world but unlike birds, he doesn't have selective thinking, which means he can't tell a white swan from a shiny red Adidas t-shirt. And so even humans can easily become part of the food chain and alas, this time not quite on top. A bird will selectively pick grains from hundreds of stones without even touching them once. A croc needs to have a bite first to see if it's worth his while.

Barren, dry landscape and dark red rocky shades escort us when we leave the town and head back south.

El Questro, sounding like a dust-covered town from one of Clint Eastwood's Western blockbusters, is disappointingly only a luxury paradise for affluently retired. It's on the Gibb River Road, the unsealed shortcut through the Kimberly from which we conveniently chickened out and blamed it on the impotence of our car. We're on its other end now and look for recompensation. But because we're not into El Questro at all. Emma Gorge, only a few kilometres before it, will more than do. It's only twenty-five kilometres from where we are now. I know, it doesn't sound much but on this gravel road it feels like a hundred. Emma Gorge has a wonderful natural pool and is luxury itself. Free. The waterfall there is irresistible. A wonderful refreshing place. It will be a perfect shower.

Tonight we'll be sleeping on a remote paddock about a hundred metres from the main dirt road. The field is rough and covered by hard rocky soil. We're pitching near a huge boab tree, far enough from the nearby water stream. The crocodile thoughts are not leaving us at ease.

Australia has a paradox. Despite all these vast swathes of land, there is often nowhere to put the tent up. The ground is so hard the hammer bends the metal pins. It's a bit like in cities where there's often an excess of space but nowhere to park cars. I wonder if the modern city planners borrowed inspiration from the local landscape.

The field is completely empty, except for occasional trees and dry shrubs. Every now and then a passing car raises dust clouds on the barely visible main road. The dust patiently settles back on its uneven surface each time. In the dark, the lights of an oncoming car are discernible for kilometres away.

Clouds of dust after a passing car

We know that because there are only a few cars driving that night. Bellows of free-roaming cows in the distance add some uneasiness to our pondering about what to do in such a place in case of a fire. Not an ideal place to spend a night, but what can we do? Kununurra is at least seventy kilometres away and we really need to have a good rest before heading there. For a good reason.

27
Castration as a Job: Kununurra

Kununurra grows each season by a good few thousand travelling workers on local farms, a large percentage of them backpackers. They make the local campgrounds their temporary homes. Agricultural business worth millions of dollars thrives here because of a gigantic dam that irrigates it all. They grow everything here that the tropics can offer and then sell it all over the country.

The plan is simple: find a job for a week just to keep the momentum going. No dramas. If nothing else, we'll have some extra cash for petrol. Normally you don't get to those places unless you work there, which should be another bonus. And so we sign up to a local job agency. There are a few in the town. At the moment they have a choice of watermelon picking and something calling itself *corn detasseling*.

"It's a fantastic job! Easy, easy! You're just walking all day and—and tearing down corn tops," says a young employee of the agency in some regional British accent. She points to a sample cluster hanging on the notice board.

When filling the forms out, she is polishing her nails while giggling with somebody on the phone.

It's humming with life in the camp. It feels like a community of travellers. Mainly young guys pretty much from everywhere, and all in rather shabby-looking cars, criss-crossing Australia in all directions. An Australian guy at a watermelon plantation bursts into laughter after being told what the rates are. "It was higher five years ago!" he says. "I was here then!"

We're going to work tomorrow and can't sleep. It doesn't make sense because we're tired. What's more, the couple in the neighbouring tent was already at it shortly after lunch and are at it again. Wild passionate sex with tent canvas the only barrier between us. The left tent. Now the pair from the right tent are doing the same, only louder. It starts slowly, with tender whispers, within minutes intensifying into groans, soon culminating in slaps and spanks with some dirty talk moans between rounds. That scenario will repeat itself five times in a row. Night after night. It's like one of those TV shows, you know how they will unravel, but you're lazy to grasp for the remote so you wait out the happy ending. We badly need to sleep. We're going to detassel corn tomorrow and don't in the slightest have an idea what that means. "You're going to tear down the corn tops. Easy. Very easy."

The next morning we're trudging to the agreed spot where a minibus is to take us into the field. The guy in the khaki sleeveless shirt and green cap is about fifty and the skin on his bare arms is burnt to a cinder. He is Roger, our boss. He signs everybody in and asks if we have water. Plenty of water. Five litres each—not negotiable. So early in the morning and it's incredibly hot. Like thirty-five degrees Celsius. The car turns to a dirty unpaved road after about thirty kilometres. The 4WD van doesn't have a problem with that. The driver doesn't even bother to slow down a tiny bit. A fine thin dust slowly rising from the chassis has filled the whole interior and starts to grind between teeth. We see endless fields[17] of corn. Some have rows of baby corn, not even a metre high, with sprouts in clusters; others have ripe corn, twice as high and almost ready to be taken down.

Endless cornfields of Kununurra, WA: young corn

I was used to going through corn fields when I was a boy, but never realised how much work was going into growing it. The sort cultivated here is for people's menus and the process is even fussier. In young corn, the faulty ones are those that have grown *significantly* higher than the average. They should be mercilessly eradicated, by tearing them out with the roots. In more mature corn, which might be two metres and higher, only the tops are pulled out. If that sounds too easy, there are three rows of male corn plants intercut with two rows of female corn, or something to that effect.

"Owright guys," commands Roger the foreman. "We've got irrigated rows here. They were done overnight. I recommend you take off your shoes." With that, he assigns two rows to each of us and off we go.

Feet get buried deep down in the mud. Those who left their shoes on have to pull them out of the wet brown soil by hand only after a few steps.

First, we try to understand what it is that's being asked from us—which plants are good enough to be left alone and which ones deserve attention. It's not an exact science. In fact, it's very subjective. Everybody seems to be taking them down at his or her own will, being the judge and the executioner at the same time.

The twelve-member or so team is international, a jolly bunch of young people: a chatty Irish girl on good terms with the boss, a local Australian, a couple of Scots, two Canadians and a Frenchmen who is all *"bien sûr et très bien, but foreign languages are not my cup of tea"*. Bien Sûr is however good fun and time passes faster with him. The midday break is half an hour, it's a ten-hour shift. The drink bottles stay in the van and are reachable only after finishing the rows—sometimes kilometres away. Toilets are everywhere around. Just squat and sort it out. A helicopter sometimes flies over our heads, occasionally freezing in mid-air to blow and spread the seeds out of the males to females, in the act of hybrid matchmaking and procreation in the plant world—courtesy of modern technology.

Endless cornfields of Kununurra, WA: riper corn

Detasseling is a euphemism. It slowly becomes clear that we were quite unknowingly turned into paid sadists who mercilessly castrate the male population of corn plants by pulling off their willies—or tassels—so they can still somehow spread their semen to the other variety in next rows. The more promiscuous they are, the better offspring they will produce. The eunuchs can no longer bother females in their own rows and everybody, Roger above them all, is happy.

Machines can be heard in the distance. They zip through the rows shortly before us with high speed but poor precision, and that's where our manual labour comes in. Roger disappears from sight but frequently reappears from nowhere to say, "Good, good. You people better do it slowly and well."

Okay, no problem.

At six in the evening, we're driven back to our makeshift homes. Our sweaty bodies are covered in pollen, we've been stung by mosquitoes and our hands are covered in tiny scratches from palm to neck. We're greeted by guys who were picking watermelons all day.

"Corn? Fucking piece of cake, mate! Watermelons—you bend all day, pick and handle heavy loads, and there are spiders, mice and other uglies everywhere."

Great, what a relief I'm thinking, scratching my itchy crotch. The pollen is very fine and gets everywhere. Some people don't mind it at all, others might have an extreme reaction. After the first day of work, the itch takes the sleep away, and so does the loud sex in the neighbouring tent.

On the fourth day, the work doesn't go as fast. Roger is accompanied by his superior, who looks like a big wig from the company who normally manages everything from his desk somewhere, and makes everybody around him look small and insignificant. Including Roger. He walks everywhere with him and makes wild gestures. In today's rows, defects are on almost every plant. The machinist before us must have been drunk or something and so there are plenty of fixes. I'm doing what I was told to do a few days ago—I am slow but thorough—to me, it's business as usual. The only person I see is Bien Sûr, who I use as a benchmark; a walking evidence that I am not the slowest one, although all the others have all but disappeared from sight. He's got headphones in his ears to take the pain out of the work, and overall looks very cool and relaxed.

But only a moment later Roger materialises out of our nowhere, saying, "You guys buggered or what? You'd better not come tomorrow, mate," after which he quickly disappears again, but not before walking to the next row where he delivers the same message to my French neighbour.

Bien Sûr is completely at ease, consumed by his world of music, and categorically not letting anyone disturb that harmony and peace. The next morning he comes to work like normally, only to be told officially in front of everybody, "YOU'RE FIRED!"

28
Sea in the Desert: Lake Argyle

From Kununurra, it is only a short distance to Lake Argyle, one of the largest man-made water reservoirs in Australia. Its size and capacity are so vast that it could fit Sydney Harbour twenty-six times.

Lake Argyle dam,[18] WA

It was finished in 1972, and what used to be hilltops are now seventy or so islands. It's surrounded by a magnificently picturesque terrain and the colours at sunset on a local boat cruise are nothing short of splendid. The small boat goes to the all attractions one by one, and the guide is confident we're going to see them all. First, the rock-wallabies slowly moving around the reddish cliffs, then fresh-water crocodiles lying motionless at the shore, before jumping to water in a splinter of a second when the boat gets too close, next are golden orb spiders who make their webs in the dry treetops. Their spider webs are so strong they can even catch small birds. NASA is said to have used them for their exceptional properties in the space suits research program, until the suits began to resemble cocoons. But there are also spitting fish. Just drop a few breadcrumbs in the water and they will hurl small streams of water back at you. They think you are insects and want to eat you. I bet you those weren't in any research program.

Golden orb spiders in dry treetops

At sunset, it's time to open wines and beers and go for a swim in the lake. The number of crocodiles here is around twenty-five thousand but hey, don't worry! "The freshie is a goodie, mate. Grab a pool noodle and jump in!" The fresh-water crocodile is said to be "harmless unless you start to mess with it. Then you can end up armless, that's what it is" continues a jolly woman guide in her forties. What a relief. The water is beautiful and warm. It's evening but it's not cold at all. Or another comparison: "play with a fresh-water crocodile and all you need is microsurgery. Play with a saltie and all you need is a wooden box."

Tom and Ellyssa are a couple who love travel. He used to work for a large high-tech company for fifteen years until it was swallowed up by a larger high-tech company, and that in turn was devoured by an even larger high-tech predator. He was one of the gnawed away bones that fell off the fresh corporate carcass. He didn't mind much in the end because he got a nice redundancy package and was sick of them all anyway. They bought a caravan and set out for some serious travels. She works from home and they have no children. Their caravan looks better than most luxurious city flats.

Fresh-water crocodile

"Backpackers, eh?" says a giant bearded guy standing next to us selling beer at a small stall counter. When he's not doing that, he works as a local ranger—a nice chap with grumpy humour, not exactly talkative, but after two beers his tongue is coming loose. It turns out he's not just a ranger. He is a part of a water protection program, as he puts, "an anti-terrorist thing".

"When you take into account how big this lake is, somebody not in his right senses might come one day and sabotage it." There was a moment of silence. He didn't say it exactly how but what he meant was probably poisoning the lake.

Now some people really are weird, but how much of a crackpot would you have to be to venture into the middle of a lake that is one hundred kilometres long and eighty kilometres wide in a completely inaccessible wasteland during a forty-two degree scorcher carrying—how much of the lethal stuff would you need—and then try escape as the first terrorist in history to solo-cross the Kimberleys and then the sea on the way to your base somewhere in Asia. Make no mistake. You would not make it.

But hey, we get it. This guy has just been back from his OH&S meeting: Occupational Health and Safety. Those meetings are compulsory everywhere now, they feel like they'll never end and one of the hardest things at workplaces today is not to fall asleep during one of them.

He is measuring us from head to toe while squinting, making us feel uncomfortable. He has been given the authority to remove anyone who poses a threat to the lake.

Lake Argyle at night

"I am telling you, go this way, that's fine," he says quietly and he stretches his right hand. "But don't go this way," he says even more mysteriously and he stretches his left arm. After telling him that we actually are terrorist and we did come to demolish the lake and could he please point us to the fastest escape route, he suddenly goes solemn-faced and shouts, "Two of my friends died in Bali and I will see to it we'll have none of that here!"

"Gee," whispers the other Australian at the table. "What's got into him?" And he quickly changes subject to fishing.

The government rents this campground for short periods, usually one year, after which the license must be renewed. As a result, the area remains pristine. The campground is basic and worn-down, and there is no effort to attract crowds. Three people are enjoying the warm pool.

"Now, do you want to see A FISH? We have silver cobblers here." Standing to his feet, he opens a huge outdoor freezer and a large five-kilo rock-solid frozen fish is out sitting on the table top. Its wide-open sparkling eyes are staring at us as if they wanted to tell us a story. If not for a bit of frost lying on its head, I swear I would think it's alive. The silver cobbler is a star. It used to have a boring name, shovel-nosed catfish, but the food marketers changed it and it worked. It's one of the best eating fish species in Australia.

Australia has mystery spots. You can still access some with determination and luck, but many are reserved for a select few.

Parts of Lake Argyle might be in that category. In spite of its remoteness, it's a strategic place. And it's not just water. Diamonds were discovered in its southern part in Matsu Range in around 1970. With a single mine, Australia suddenly found itself in the prestigious club of top diamond producers, making one third of the world's production. Some of the diamonds are of pinkish colour and outstanding quality. It goes without saying that they don't want you and me sniffing around. And it's not exactly a place with public transport either, so even getting to the first gate might pose a problem of its own. It can be found on the Google map but only in satellite view[19]. Apparently it spans across Aboriginal sacred site called Barramundi Gap. Rio Tinto, a large mining multinational, now owns the domain.

Other parts of the lake are known for the discovery of an interesting stone called zebra rock. It's not a gemstone but it's not found anywhere else in the world and, as the name suggests, it looks exactly like zebra skin. It was forming by layers of sediment for about six hundred million years. Quite impressive when you think dinosaurs left 'only' about sixty-five million years ago.

We're meeting our ranger friend the next morning on the dam road shortly before leaving. He slows down, opens his window and mumbles, "So, you're leaving eh?" After getting some nods from us, he goes on, "Good on ya, bloody backpackers."

29
Customs and Public Holidays: Northern Territory Border

It's about an hour's drive from Lake Argyle to the border with Northern Territory. Crossing into the Northern Territory is like leaving a richer country for a poorer one, predominantly for one reason. The Western Australians will turn your car upside down. not in search of drugs and weapons but in search of fruits and veggies. *Fruitcake police.* Your car must be free of anything that might host fruit flies. If somebody smuggled them over the border they could render Roger and his boss instantaneously unemployed. Therefore there are big penalties and each agricultural business boasts the fly-free zone status. It can even show on some maps. If one single bastard fly is found, the certification and paperwork would force businesses dig deep into their pockets. So, the Western Australians got this sorted and everybody is happy. Right? Well, apparently not quite. "We Northern Territory farmers would like those checks too." Bad luck. They are few and far between and their lobby is weak.

The one-way border moves your clock forward by one and a half hours. This may seem like an interesting oddity, but it is not unusual given that hardly anybody lives here. A more interesting example can be found in Coolangatta, Queensland, a town bordering New South Wales, where a busy Gold Coast airport is located. From October to April, half of the town is on a different time zone due to daylight savings. It is 10 a.m. on one side of the street but 11 a.m. on the other. Not all Australian states use daylight saving time changes.

The next twenty-four-hour rest place looks great, like always. There is smoke from fireplaces. Strange because it's very dry tonight and a fire ban might be in force.

A thirty-odd-year-old caravan stands nearby. The owner's name is Ken, and it's not long before he sits at our fireplace. He used to drive with his wife; now, unfortunately, he's driving alone.

He is from the older generation of gentlemen who are always nice to talk to. He brought us his potatoes because the next day they would be confiscated. He's going to WA. And so we're putting the spuds in the fire to bake and talk about times gone by.

His father was injured four times: once in Gallipoli, where the British so graciously sent their Australian and New Zealand cousins to the firing line. Rather than holding a grudge, they turned it into a cornerstone of the new national identity—a legend that on April 25 each year is celebrated as ANZAC Day. They got a day off.

In 1914, when Australia was only thirteen years old, the old chums from Britain came here and said, "Howdy! There is a war out there, and we would appreciate your help in blowing up Germans in their dens. You don't have to, of course, but if *you* get busy one day, you might not have an ally. Just look north. Fifty times as many enemies are waiting at the gates. Good luck. God bless."

A desperate soldier in a Canberra museum

A strange campaign started. Poor families of new settlers were visited by army recruiters promising adventures to their sons. Young boys in scruffy shorts were listening to a nicely dressed army officials' stories of the big world. "Do you want to travel around the globe, lad? Join us! We'll train you, son. You'll see big things. You'll help your country, your dad, your mom. You'll become a hero." The youngsters, looking at the bleak outlook of their immediate future, often said yes. The officials didn't mind that many of them were only sixteen or seventeen. They recruited about fifty thousand in Australia and about eighteen thousand of them in New Zealand. Many were sent to Asia Minor to pacify Turks, and in a selfless act of patriotism, to seize Istanbul. During landing, however, things went awry. By that time however Turks really had it with the Monarchy and massacred Australians with machine-guns. With big losses on both sides, the British enventually called it a day after eight months of pointless fighting.

Countries like to be built on memorials. The last ANZAC hero passed away in 2002. His name was Alec Campbell and he was one hundred and three years old.

30
Spa Time: Katherine is Hot, Douglas is Cool

People we know in Katherine live about twenty kilometres outside the town. They grow mangos and mahogany trees. The latter takes a long time but makes for a fine export item. It's used for furniture and acoustic guitars. A small forest is on the hill because floods are here almost every year.

The narrow road to their house is full of kangaroos. They don't even bother to move away. John and Jane have two hounds. They use them to chase them and occasionally finish off the Australian icons right in the street, practically in front of their neighbours' small children. Something like a hobby. When asking them if it's not cruel to kill a cute plush animal like a roo, they only shake their heads in disbelief, "this bloody pest, you mean?"

Their house is a typical tropical dwelling with large windows and large bushy unkempt garden. A huge green frog is sitting on the porch. Both of them live off the farm but she makes extra money by teaching math and he makes social programs for the local Aboriginal community. Children have flown out of the nest and study somewhere in a remote city. Both are very well educated.

"Katherine Gorge is a beautiful place. You should go there. And don't miss the *hot springs* in the town," they say.

Knowing locals is always worth gold. They point you to places you normally don't find. Like Scout Hall. "Go off the Victoria Highway to Rundle Street and then to Campbell Terrace till you reach the end at Riverbank Drive." It is not hot but pleasantly warm. It's a natural pool with thirty-four degrees Celsius crystal clear water. It's not thermal, it's not volcanic, it is simply warmed by the earth and gushes out to the top. Pure ingenuity of nature. One could bathe all day in it. An ideal place after a long journey. In the wet season, the water level can rise by fifteen metres, then it's all under water.

While sitting in this little waterhole, there is a family with two pre-adolescent sons. For two years now, they've been touring Australia in a caravan, setting up equipment for karaoke shows in pubs. Karaoke is quite popular in the country and Australians treat their artistic performances rather seriously. Performers are rewarded with hefty applause, and for a while everybody can be a music star. The caravan is long and tows a small car behind it. Whenever they're free they pan for gold with a metal detector in the outback. They show us samples. Some of that is fools gold, but there are also a few large nuggets. Children do home schooling. They pass some exams from time to time and off they go again. They wouldn't change this lifestyle for anything, because, as the happy father puts it, "Look at the beauty around. It's all my garden. And this here is my spa!"

Not far from here is Katherine Gorge, part of the Nitmiluk National Park where many interesting tracks start along the river; for instance the fourteen-kilometre long Butterfly Gorge.

Cascading waterfalls at Edith Falls, going for miles and miles through perfect solitude

Into the third kilometre and still not a soul around. The river goes on but the track gradually ends and we would need a canoe. We're following along the rocky walls as far as we can, sometimes crossing water and having a good swim. Water here is so nice.

A snake is going up a tree and another one is resting on a big rock in front. Colourful butterflies are all around.

"By the way, last week two large crocs were spotted. They got one of them, but the other is still at large somewhere in the gorge," says our host at the dinner, serving food with a cheeky smile. And he takes out the local paper to prove it.

"That's okay guys. The probability is so small that we didn't want to be spoil sports. You wouldn't swim otherwise".

Edith Falls[20] are on the way to Darwin, where we're aiming for the next day, and a track there takes us up the river on cascading waterfalls to Sweetwater Pools and Upper Pools, where it feels like total isolation. The few people we meet are overseas tourists. Nobody seems to be going too far from the car park.

A local newspaper informing about crocodiles

Then it's the Stuart Highway again to take us north. It was named after a guy who, as the first European, crossed the continent from Adelaide to Van Diemen's Land. John McDuall Stuart did it in 1862 and—as was not always obvious then—he also returned.

A left turn shortly after Hayes Creek goes to Daly River and Douglas Hot Springs, also known as Tjuwaliyn[21]. The last seven kilometres of the road is dirt we're stopped by another big water patch. Just when we're turning around, another old 2WD Toyota is coming in our direction. A young ranger says he crosses the pool every day. No problems. The puddle doesn't look so bad after all, there is only one big rock hiding in the murky water.

Bumpy road to Douglas Hot Springs

Douglas Hot Springs can be hot all right. The name is not misleading. However, it is different from the one in Katherine. It is a small creek where hot water seeps from somewhere and mixes with much colder water around it. It can be really hot at some spots and rather cold in others. Small fish will approach you if you stop moving, gently touching you to see if you are edible.

There are small towns further up north like Pine Creek—nice for a stop and refreshment and Batchelor, about thirty kilometres past Adelaide River. It as an interesting landmark. A true miniature copy of Karlstein castle[22] stands at the corner of Rum Jungle Road and Tarkarri Road. The place is called Havlik Park and is named after an immigrant and adventurer who built it in 1978.

Cathedral Termite Mound is the next stop—a five-metre high pile of earth has been home to the plant-eating termites for over seventy years now.

Litchfield National Park might be taken for Kakadu's smaller brother. Everything is close here and we don't have to drive far to see it all. Buley Rock Hole, for instance where cormorants show off diving and fishing skills in the waterfall. They are unbelievably fast. Florence Falls nearby is a waterfall hole with large boulders good for swimming and diving. The water is beautifully clean. Payments for the bushcamp are self-serviced.

Mosquitoes swarm in the evening and can even get through the tent netting. There is a loud bunch of yahoos camping next to us drinking and yelling late into the night. Just like sailors recognise land by squeaking sea gulls, land travellers recognise nearing cities by squeaking youngsters in camps. It simply has to be anticipated. God's mills grind slowly and surely the group is repaid in the morning. They fell asleep by the fire and the mozzies took care of them. In the morning they run around sore and itchy.

Welcoming smoke to Darwin

Fires can be spotted on the road to Darwin—the Northern Territory's capital. Sometimes even large tree trunks are in flames but that's all controlled. The landscape is dry and a large column of smoke is billowing over the city in the distance.

31
Darwin in a Nutshell

Soon we pass a large fire by the road but nobody seems to care. Back-burning routine. Fire is a part of the landscape. Darwin[23], named after the biologist, is the most populated town of the Territory and is surprisingly upbeat and modern. Two events destroyed the city in the past. Cyclone Tracy in 1974 and the Japanese bombs in 1942. Each time it was rebuilt and upgraded. It's making a fresh but sleepy impression. Streets are wide, the centre of it looking out into a large bay is nice and clean. It's one of those places where people come to live temporarily—two, three years and then they move on.

A music festival is in the town right now and it's buzzing with artists and performers everywhere, small groups of alternative music from all around the world. We're watching them sing and dance while we lie on the park lawn. Hippie, relaxed vibe under open sky, colourful dresses, beads, flowers, exotic food scent and perfect climate. Mindil Beach Sunset Market seems to have all this kind of alternative lifestyle can offer. The music goes on till the late evening. The name got it right. Sunset here is amazing. A fire can be seen far in the distance on the other side of the bay. The crowded Shady Glen Caravan Park feels like a hotel after all those rough nights.

Having replenished supplies it's time for the local nude beach. The water is warm, the sea incredibly beautiful. There are white cone-shaped shells everywhere. Walking naked in the sea a few hundred metres with water still only knee-deep is a strange feeling especially that a croc was spotted here a few times in the past.

Hidden Valley camp is much cleaner and less busy. It's time to head south again. But before that, let's explore Kakadu, the largest national park in Australia the size of a small country.

After twenty-nine days on the road, we've travelled six and a half thousand kilometres and have approximately nine thousand more to reach Sydney.

IV. Darwin to Alice Springs

32
Where You Only Swim in a Pool: Kakadu

Sitting on a boat behind a thick acrylic glass panel, we observe a piece of hanging meat. It's going above a water surface that is unusually calm, with only a few innocent ripples. Then, as if in a nanosecond, that calmness takes the shape of a four-metre reptile beast and the meatloaf disappears under water with a loud snatch. It's fast and it comes from nowhere. A crocodile farm on the way to the park offers this as a paid tourist attraction.

There is only one bitumen road going through the whole area that is as big as a small country. All other roads are 4x4 dirt roads.

"Mate, the only place you can swim here is a swimming pool in Jabiru," says a chatty Aboriginal guide in the Bowali Visitor Centre. The realisation of what a formidable creature a crocodile can be has been coming to us gradually since first entering the northern parts of Western Australia. Here you can buy a tooth as a souvenir. It's basically a miniature of a dagger. There are about seventy of them in a row; like a saw that crushes its prey with a pressure comparable only to that of a hydraulic press. Apparently, the jaw's grip is forty times stronger than the human's.

It isn't long before I ask why Kakadu isn't dubbed Moskidu. The omnipresent mosquitoes don't work night shifts but they are 24/7, like street lights. They will get everywhere—be it a tent or a car. Unlike their European *rellies*, or relatives, who normally wait till dusk, then gently and secretly enter your blood bank, steal a bit of jewelry, wipe out tracks and disappear, this kind unscrupulously perpetrates open burglary in daylight, doesn't care about noise or being shot, and completely empties your safe, after devastating the whole bloody unit. Only entomologists know why it is so, but I bet this blood-guzzling quirk of evolution is the equivalent of a croc in the insect world. It can be five millimetres long and look like a stuck pin when it's dining off you.

When pitching a tent in the Malabanjbandju Caravan Area, we rub our hands at how clever we are, finding such a nice free camping spot even though we can't pronounce its name. What a peaceful place this park is. But after a short walk through the jungle of the East Alligator River, things start to look differently. A big warning board makes no mistake about it: "Danger. Crocodiles inhabit this area. Attacks cause injury or death." Succinct but clear.

It's their home and their territory.

Crocodile warning sign

Once in the bush by the river, mozzies loom from nowhere and attack without warning. Ten minutes and I am itchy, run back to the car for a repellent, and in all that commotion, somehow lock myself out. The car key is smirking through the rear window, only a few centimetres from the glass. How am I going to get to them now?"

What follows is a weak attempt to break into my own car. I have hardly any skills in that area so the only other thing I can think of is a heavy spanner borrowed from occupants of the nearby van. The small rear window is the main casualty of that incident but it's a tough little bugger. It won't go without a fight. It's unbelievably hard and shatters only after three mighty hits.

Glass fragments are everywhere and I am aware that the first useful junkyards will be in Adelaide and probably only in Melbourne. There are no spare parts available through the Red Centre of Australia. We'll be driving down the whole continent without one of the windows.

In a bit of stress and having nearly run over a dingo on the way back from the East Alligator River and Ubirr Rock, we trundle back to Malabanjbandju for the worst night of the whole trip, with zillions of mosquitoes filling the space of the provisional campsite to the very last cubic inch. They make air raids into face: ears, nose, eyes; you name it. We can't eat, and so try to hide in the car but they've got there already through the broken window. Finally we zip shut the tent but they're already in it, waiting in darkness. The thought of a river with crocodiles just metres away isn't making this any easier.

In Jabiru the next morning, the only pool in the area is closed. It's too early. It's time for Nourlangie Rock—a place with Aboriginal paintings on rock walls—quite a popular place. Visitors arrive in vans but not many of them walk the full loop track that goes around the rock: Barrk Sandstone Walk. The information board says it's going to take six to eight hours. That's three and a half hours of normal walking speed. It takes us up a steep hill for an outlook of Kakadu and goes back to the valley near the Nourlangie Rock Art Site[24]. We meet people there again who admire the paintings that—no matter if authentic or restored—are a good attraction for tourists and food for thought. They are said to be one of the oldest human records of its kind in the world, dating back as far as almost thirty thousand years ago.

Aboriginal paintings at Barrk Sandstone, NT

It is only about fifty kilometres from Nourlangie to Cooinda—a small settlement that will do for the night. Yellow Water with river cruises is not far from here, as well as Sandy Billabong, a place of a sad tragedy, that at first might be a bit hard to comprehend.

33
Of Crocodiles and Men: Take II

During a hot night in the middle of tourist season, nine young backpackers with a guide are camping near Sandy Billabong. The air is hot, humid and muggy. You can't do much on those days, and thoughts circle around where you could dip in water to cool down. And this little creek nearby reflecting the moon on its surface looks so inviting. While one of them is trying to play didgeridoo, the guide Glenn has just finished washing up and rubs the sweat drops off his forehead.

"Swim, anybody?" He got their attention but they looked at one another, rather puzzled.

What about crocs? As far as he knows there shouldn't be any around here. Often he used to see Aboriginal people swimming in this kind of waterholes. Surely somebody must have been here before them because he sees some mussels lying around. This is too far from the sea for any saltie and the freshies are shy. Still, they ask him a few more times for reassurance.

The guide is experienced, it can't be his first tour and he must have done this many times before. He points his torch to water and can't see any danger. Then he jumps in the water and swims. Others take off their clothes and follow. The billabong is full of happy cheers and splashing fun. It's full moon, and if not for intrusive mosquitoes it might feel like paradise.

"I have to check on the next group," gestures the guide and slowly leaves water. The party goes on. Some people start to go further and deeper down the pond. When the twenty-three-year-old Isabel screams and disappears under the surface, nobody takes this seriously. When she re-emerges, her lungs are already punctured and the crocodile starts to mercilessly pull her under water. Everybody gets it by now but cannot do anything. They run out of the water in panic and scream for help. It's an ugly and chaotic scene. More people arrive and a search party is organised that finally spots and puts the crocodile to death. When they salvage the body, they shortly brush with another croc.

It's not a made-up story. It's the 22 October 2002.

The autopsy confirms that the first attack was not fatal. Crocodiles usually kill by drowning and this time wasn't any different. Ironically the croc has a damaged jaw and wouldn't live long.

The victim's sister and all the others suffered a shock of their lives in a tragedy that in the papers reads only as another sensational curiosity.

34
Flying in the Bush: Mataranka

The next day, the Kakadu Highway takes us back to the Stuart Highway - the main corridor to the south. As we kill off the few mosquitoes that have somehow survived in the car, we start to think about what's next. Since we have to pass through Katherine again, the choice is obvious: the wonderful natural spa called Scouts Hall, which we've been to before. But what's next?

"At least it doesn't stink and you don't get shat on your head," say two people who must have been frolicking in the water long before we arrived.

"By who?" we ask.

"The bats," they reply.

"But where?" we ask again.

"In Mataranka," they say.

Mataranka, Mataranka. We know our next destination.

Mataranka[25] is a place that the locals talk about with a bit of hesitation in their voice. It's nice, but no thanks.

The water springs are thirty-four degrees Celsius: in our opinion there is no stench and if there is, it's bearable. What makes this place great, however, is the occasional presence of bats.

Personally, we were expecting to see a few hundred of them, not more, and that would make a day for us. So when we walk into the local pub looking for a place to stay, we're pointed in the direction of the Mataranka campground.

"But they're here now," the guy says, not lowering his eyes from the TV screen and chewing something.

"Yeah, that's no problem, we don't mind."

"Two and a half million of them," he adds, his eyes still glued to the screen.

What's even better is that when the sun goes down, which will be in about three hours, they'll all take off, heading for the nightlife somewhere far away from here.

After coffee we are at the gate to Elsey National Park.

The palm forest is busy. *Pteropus*, the flying fox, also known as the fruit bat, is the largest bat species in the world. Adults can reach a wingspan of almost two metres.

Bats of Mataranka taking off for night-life

Some of them hang motionless from palm leaves, others fly restlessly from branch to branch, pushing and shoving each other and generally fighting for the last bit of space left because the palm bush is so overparked that even a small gap on the trunk is an opportunity to find some shade and have a rest.

They use their huge wings as fans to cool themselves, and their screeches—a cross between apes and birds—echo far into the ether. In the middle of it all is a pool of crystal-clear water at a temperature just below that of the human body. Once in, you don't want to leave.

"Isn't this cool? We were in Sydney this only morning and now this," say two middle-aged gentlemen splashing in water.

We ask them how on earth it is even possible—to get here so quickly from Sydney. It's at least like three and a half thousand kilometres.

"We flew in. There's an airstrip over there," and he reluctantly reaches his hand out of the warm water to show a field beyond the trees.

"Our plane is over there," says the second pointing in another direction.

Later that evening, over live music in the local pub, two ex-Qantas pilots tell us how they are flying to Darwin to sell a YAK-52 light aircraft to a private club consisting of eight members. It's been sourced somewhere in Ukraine, imported, then refurbished for Australian standards and it is now ready for delivery. Mataranka is just a stop-over.

"It's the best value for money aircraft you can get your hands on," they explain further.

"The syndicate put the funds together."

"Russian planes are the best, mate," says the other.

"You can cobble them together in your yard. The Americans put all sorts of useless electronic shit in their planes. Who knows what's what?"

"This here? Beauty. A piece of cake."

The guys seem to know their stuff. One of them travelled to Russia a lot on business. He once had to take the wife of one of his business partners, a never-been-out-of-her-suburb type of woman as he puts it, and act as her guide in Moscow. As he showed her the city's major attractions, from Red Square to St Basil's Cathedral to the Kremlin, he also took her to the mausoleum—the *Lenin's tomb*.

And hey, she was really impressed!"

Because she didn't know "that John Lennon was buried in Moscow!"

"I almost pissed my pants," he chuckles.

Kangaroos walk around the tents at night and our voyeuristic channel broadcasts another episode. Loud passionate sex can be heard from a nearby tent.

We got up early so we wouldn't miss the plane taking off. Two silhouettes stand next to an open bonnet, fiddling with something in the engine. The preparations are thorough. The plane itself looks like it has just come off the assembly line. The Mataranka airstrip is full of kangaroos grazing on the dew-covered grass, unaware that in about an hour they'll be chased by a flying machine doing a hundred kilometres an hour.

YAK-52 on the Mataranka airstrip, NT

Finally, the pilots wave goodbye and take off. It takes a few minutes for them to climb and turn, then to descend and fly over the heads of the cheering crowd. The crowd waves back. They don't see us anymore and their dot in the sky gets smaller and smaller until it disappears completely.

35
Alice in Wander Land

A long stretch of road awaits us from Mataranka south—about 580 kilometres to Mary Ann Dam. There is not much to see but it's still quite a nice drive. At times the road follows the railway line that cuts through Australia to the south and where the scenic Ghan rushes to Adelaide. It's one hell of a long straight rail track.

Daly Waters[26] offers a nice stop—a 'shithouse' pub with hundreds of souvenirs scattered around its walls—coins, notes, bits of underwear, money from all around the world, hats, shirts with messages all hanging next to each other in a silent testimony of the number of people who have visited this place before us. Outside is a wooden latrine with an old guitar hanging on it.

"Shithouse" in Daly Waters, NT

After Daly Waters, a sign indicates something called Churchill Hat—apparently a rock reminiscent of Churchill with his famous cigar. It's as good as having a break anyway, so let's check this out. There is nothing even close to looking like a cigar, let alone Churchill. In the local terminology, somebody is just taking the piss or has vivid imagination.

Elliot[27] is a place with a large Aboriginal population. The day is very hot and people linger in whatever shade they can find.

"Sucks to be doing that in this heat, mate," one of them says to a white maintenance man balancing on a ladder, changing a light bulb at the local petrol station.

"He don't mind, he's getting paid," says the other.

Stray dogs don't want to leave us alone so we push on. Renner Springs offers Free Coffee for Driver and it comes handy.

Three Ways, about twenty kilometres before Tennant Creek, is a place that all serious travellers know quite well. It's a crossing, as the name suggests and a decision has to be made here to go Alice Springs South or to Townsville East.

Road trains park at the roadhouse. They have three and more trailers and are about forty metres long. They are only allowed in remote areas, carry all kinds of stuff and trailers have to detach before entering larger townships.

Nothing special at Mary Ann Dam except a free but cold shower. Another APC night: Arms, Pits and Crotch.

There are three other caravans, so it seems safe. The ground is unbelievably hard, with patches of sharp, prickly thorns called bindis. If they were alive, they would say to you: *"Bugger off! Hurt your fingers you idiot! We hate tents!"* But we don't listen and pitch it anyway, like every day.

Tomorrow's distance to Alice Springs is short. Only about 530 kilometres.

Old car wrecks near Tennant Creek, NT

After a casual drop to Tennant Creek, we're getting closer to a remarkable place called Karlu Karlu,[28] better known as the Devils Marbles—thousands of large boulders and rock formations strewn across a relatively small patch of land. They are the remnants of a huge rock mass that fell apart millions of years ago, actively assisted by water and wind, who first made cracks in them and then let them crumble into thousands of pieces. Some of them look like they're arranged on one another, round and sculptured, as if deliberately split in half, and all of that is said to lie on a massive and intact mega-sized boulder buried deep in the ground. This is how the big monolith of Uluru is going to look in a few million years.

A little bit more south and we're in Barrow Creek, which is not so much a place to stop as a part of road where the much publicised case of Peter Falconio played out in 2001. He travelled with his girlfriend Joanne Lees from Darwin to Alice. At night, they were stopped by Bradley John Murdoch who was to kill him and kidnap her. And we only know because she managed to escape. Anyway, this was exactly the kind of inspiration that the Australian horror filmmakers were waiting for.

Karlu Karlu / The Devils Marbles, NT

The landscape suddenly becomes hilly. We're at the threshold to Alice Springs—the imaginary centre of Australia—and Wintersun Caravan Park is our first refuge. Alice has about fourteen thousand inhabitants and many, many, many more flies.

Later, on the same day, we see Anzac Hill with a beautiful outlook of the town

The town has a nice mix of people and we hear about *noodling* for the first time because here somewhere starts a land of opal—hydrated silica gemstones that have been mined in these parts for decades.

The Alice Springs Telegraph Station remembers almost all the modern history—an invention that enabled sending lightning speed electronic messages only ten years after Europeans settled there. Larapinta Trail starts right next to it and is a daring two hundred and something kilometre long walking track going west. The dry riverbed of the Todd River is its first section.

36
Road to Nowhere: West MacDonnell Ranges

After a short stop in Alice, it's time to check the beautiful mountain range to the west. West MacDonnell Ranges have a red beauty and look distant and solitary.

There are gaps between hilltops, where running creeks can be found most of the time. They've been water sources for thousands of years, and the reason for clashes between the European cattle grazers and the natives. Because of harsh conditions, settlers arrived only a few decades later. Things were as bad there as anywhere else, but the local Arrernte people were luckier at least in one regard. Their Aboriginal customs and life were documented better than any other tribe in Australia, thanks to two people: Francis James Gillen, who worked as an operator at the telegraph station, and Sir Walter Baldwin Spencer, an anthropologist interested in the subject. They gathered a large collection of facts and pictures and published them in a book. Everywhere else in Australia, changes were too rapid for anybody to make more detailed observations of Aboriginal ways of life.

Standley Chasm is one such gap with a paid entry but Simpsons Gap[29], about eighteen kilometres from Alice, is free. There is so much to see in Australia for free.

Chasm: a place where water chiselled mountains, NT

Driving from the Ochre Pits to Ormiston Gorge[30] takes us almost to the end of the paved road, and we stay in Ormiston Campground. Going on with a conventional car from here is not recommended.

A nice couple from South Australia say they prefer a tent to a caravan because they feel younger this way.

"When you're in South Australia, drop in. We're going to show you our farm." We jot down their address.

West MacDonnell Ranges have walking tracks like nowhere else. Pound Walk, for instance, is about an eight-kilometre-long track along a hill crest. Large boulder area towards the end of the track makes an impression of being twice as large because the rock walls mirror against the perfectly calm water surface. We have just walked into a highest-definition, 3D picture.

Perfect symmetry of the Pound Walk, NT

A howling dingo wakes us at night, and for the first time we notice cooler temperatures.

Mount Sonder is our next goal. We need to get to the base first, which for us might represent a bigger problem than the climb itself. We ask the ranger about the road quality, then point to our car.

"Sure, no problem. It's a good road," is his answer.

Eleven kilometres of the paved road really is okay, then a typical bumpy corrugated road, but there are another twenty-five kilometres of much harder surface following that, and the ending near the provisional car park at Redbank Gorge, at the foot of the mountain, is for experienced 4WD enthusiasts. No kidding. We have to leave the car about a kilometre from the destination. The road has deep recesses and in turns goes up- and downhill steeply.

The information board estimates the hike to take eight hours. It's sixteen kilometres return and it's not marked very well. After an hour's ascent it starts to dawn on us how small and insignificant we are in the vast, wide-open terrain. We almost lose sight of each other among thousands of rocks. A person only a hundred metres away perfectly merges with the surroundings and can no longer be seen. Now tell me something about efficiency of plane rescues. Let's stick together. The next five kilometres is a crest walk to the summit.

And those flies, flies and flies, everywhere, the most annoying kind that exists on the surface of this planet. If one lands on your eyelash, your hand instinctively moves to pluck it off, but to them this is an invitation; there are ten more on it now, and the one on the eyelash is still sitting undisturbed and licking diligently. This is when you may be excused to wear a fly net. It's pain in the neck in itself but the lesser of two evils.

Mount Sonder / Rwetyepme, NT: 1,380 m ASL

The summit is well worth the effort. The scenery around is unlike anything else. Standing in the middle of it, all you see is a landscape carved by nature over millions of years. The terrain defies logic and pattern: it's a total chaos of shapes and breathtaking harmony at the same time. Hundreds of miles of nothing, where people are as rare as hen's teeth.

Mount Sonder is the last section of the Larapinta Trail that started at the Telegraph Station in Alice. For a moment, we feel like we did it all.

A good walker will take five and a half hours instead of the suggested eight, but it's getting dark by the time we get back. If we're unlucky and get a flat tyre now, we'll stay here for the night. We left a torch in the tent. A fundamental mistake. The darkness here is pitch black. You don't see a thing.*

We have to replace a slowly leaking tyre in Alice, and replenish supplies. The Ghan Museum[31] is not far away, with a few fine steam locomotives on display. The Old Ghan was going through towns where there is no paved road today and where only a handful of people now live permanently. Ghan is a short for Afghan, to remember the Afghans who facilitated the first camel trains for expeditions linking the north with the south of Australia through the Red Centre. The British Empire had its resources everywhere around the globe then and that's when the telegraph came in handy.

"Kabul? Stop. Pls send camels. Stop. Horses turn to popcorn. Stop."

Not far from Alice, on a camel farm, we try to imagine how hard this exercise must have been. After only a few-minutes ride, the bum starts to collect bruises. Poor rider comfort, however, is the trade off for extremely economical performance. It's the only means of transport that runs on water. Amazingly, it gulps 120 litres of water on the spot, burps, and then walks for a week, with heavy burdens loaded all around its back, without a single thought about being thirsty.

Old Ghan not far from Alice Springs

We swap the camel back for our hatchback and head for the next right turn. After two and a half hours, we're there. We get set for the night because it's getting dark. Uluru is still around 250 kilometres away. Erldunda Caravan Park is an ideal place to prepare for one of the most enigmatic places in Australia. It's also the first time we meet Alex.

37
On a Bike Through Desert

"Where have you come from?" we ask a fit young guy, expecting a large Australian city as an answer.

"London."

"Pardon?"

"From London."

"On a bike? How long did that take?"

"About five months," replies a very modest-looking Singaporean.

Alex is doing a round trip of the world on his trekking bike and he started in London. Australia from north to south is his penultimate section. The last one will be New Zealand.

He paid a speeding ticket in Romania once, apparently the only country in the world where police fined cyclists for speeding because fines were bigger than their monthly salaries. On the other hand, the only place he could not ride were parts of China where he didn't get a permit. He was bitten by dogs a few times. A stray Fido took him down from his bike once and got a good taste of his butt. He had punctured about twenty-five tyres and had constant breakdowns but he's been patiently fixing every one of them with the tools in his small box.

Alex is tired. We can see that. Driving is easy. You sit and watch scenery. But stop and get out. Even on a sunny day, all across the outback, on this endless plateau, you will feel a mild but steady wind that's there all the time. Its only purpose is to give you hell of a hard time if you're on a pushbike.

Unlike Brian who had a bob trailer, Alex has only his bike and a backpack. Inside it, his small stove, gas container, kettle and other necessities to get by and survive. Going around Australia on a bike is easier said than done, that's for sure.

A cyclist on a ride around Australia on the Stuart Highway[32]

"I'm not turning to Uluru," says Alex. "Five hundred kilometres is too much of a detour for a bike."

"Then we'll see you again in three days."

"Three days are not enough," he says after a pause. "That's Uluru, Kings Canyon, Kata Tjuta."

"We only want to spare two nights."

"Well, good luck then. I am telling you. Not enough time."

V. New Look At the Red Centre

38
Where Things Howl: Uluru aka Ayers Rock

Our Swedish friends have warned us. The rangers will not tolerate you sleeping in popular tourist spots. They will wake you up at four in the morning and wave goodbuy to you until you disappear from sight. Complete isolation or not, this is a national park: Sleeping on the road is not allowed.

We're planning to do all three—Uluru, Kata Tjuta also know as the Olgas, and Kings Canyon—for as little money as possible. It's a very touristy place and it might be quite an ambush on the wallet. Internet searches produce endless lists of resorts and restaurants and that is the last thing we're after.

We stop at the Mount Ebenezer Roadhouse, where there is an art exhibition by local artists. An Aboriginal woman, writing on a notice board, expresses her doubts about the authorities' efforts to restrict climbing on the sacred rock, which they attribute mainly to Aboriginal opposition. According to her it has more to do with safety and preventing injuries and deaths, which nobody wants, especially the local Aboriginal community.

"False Uluru": Atilla / Mount Conner,[33] NT

Not long after leaving Mount Ebenezer, the silhouette of a large flat mountain appears on the horizon. Atilla, also known as Mount Conner, is a 'false Uluru'. It's big and impressive, even from the road. It's an *inselberg*, or island mountain, and it's remarkable because the top is what Australia was like many millions of years ago. The land around it simply eroded away, knowing that people would one day need flat roads to transport tourists in air-conditioned buses on five-hour journeys from Alice Springs.

Atilla is the last soldier standing. There is no public access to it because it's in the middle of a private cattle station called Curtin Springs. Technically speaking, it's a big rockery in somebody's giant garden.

Desert art on the way to Red Centre[34]

The tourist money machine revolves around the one the rock next: a well-recognisable image icon that stands above all others. It is a place that everybody knows.

Uluṟu and Kata Tjuṯa were returned to the traditional owners as part of the native title to land policies. Their cultural heritage for Australia is so significant that the Aborigines leased the area to government for ninety-nine years back in 1985. In the 1980s, one could come here and freely camp at its very base. It's unthinkable today.

A half-naked local woman is dancing on the film screen of the classy cultural centre, set up in the close vicinity of the Rock. There are lots of handmade high-quality wooden souvenirs that, although nothing like the tawdry rubbish in city markets, are rather expensive. Interesting pictures and facts are shown on the walls. Some of them are covered because Aboriginal culture holds showing deceased persons' photographs, voices or even names as disrespectful. When driving around the Rock, small, slowly-moving, ant-like characters are recognisable against the blue sky horizon. They go from where the climbing track starts to the top. When it's too hot, too wet or there are otherwise unfavourable conditions, the access is closed. We are lucky. The Uluru climb track will permanently close in October 2019.

There is not a cloud in the sky today. The rock is impressive, but the artificial infrastructure that surrounds it is from another world and another era.

'Car sunset viewing area', 'Car sunrise viewing area', 'Bus sunset viewing area', 'Bus sunrise viewing area'.[35] Everything is ready.

It's afternoon and the 'Car sunset viewing area' is empty, without a soul. The picture is like a postcard but tourists are still showering in the hotels of Yulara. The Rock has to wait.

About twenty-seven kilometres before Yulara, there is a nameless twenty-four-hour rest place. In fact, there are a few of them on the Lasseter Highway, small, inconspicuous spots off the main road. They are unmarked, hidden behind embankments and a bit hard to find. We drive slowly. About a hundred metres past the road, down the red sand track, there is a small area with scattered dry trees, a makeshift fireplace and a rusty wreck of an old 80s car with the door wide open. Apart from that, there is not a soul around. The sun is still hot enough for a makeshift shower from our tin can. It's dark before we know it. The tent is already up, but it's not a good feeling. We're on our own, out of sight, off the main road where only a handful of cars travel at night.

The sound of a car engine wakes us at one in the morning. A quick glance out of the tent reveals a set of headlights coming our way. Stories of lost tourists come flooding back. With a pocket knife in my pocket, just in case, I cautiously greet the strangers. They are two backpackers from Austria, and after throwing more wood on the fire we chat for another hour. But we have to get up very early to catch the sunrise.

A car wreck in a hidden rest area near Yulara

The next day the Rock is completely different. There are fast-moving clouds that cast shadows like giant magic curtains, alternately revealing a wide spectrum of colours. This monolith has stood here for millions of years, through sun, rain and wind, whether now-extinct animals have walked at its foot or a coachload of overseas tourists have taken photographs of it, whether it has baked dry in the scorching sun or been drenched in torrents of water after a long storm. It's almost like a piece of art in a big open-air museum, waiting for thieves to come and steal it. We climb poles and walk on each other's heads to get that one perfect copy of the original to take home and own, to 'immortalise' the eternal for our short-lived mayfly existence. It's hilarious and embarrassingly sad and pathetic all at the same time.

Understandably, with so much beauty concentrated in one small place there is a high danger of a spontaneous artistic nuclear fusion and the government had to step in and bring it all under control. The authorities usurp the right for commercial use of the Red Centre icons imagery. Consequently, you should use no pictures of them whatsoever, either from social media, Google internet searches or any other publicly accessible source, unless you come in person, get a permit and take your own, or buy a thick, multicoloured, two-kilogram landscape photography book. Long live regulations! Who is it that owns the Rock now?

The walk up the mountain starts at the Mala Walk car park. On the wall is a plaque commemorating those who have died here, mainly from heart disease and falls. If you follow the official trail, you'll be safe. Those who fall are busybodies who tempt fate by going too far over the edge. The physical consequences are quite simple. One minute I am standing firmly on both feet, the next the ground becomes a slope, and finally the slope becomes a wall. And because I don't have bristles or suckers like insects to walk up walls, gravity takes over long before I know it. Therefore, I stay on the marked track.

The first half is a steep climb along a metal chain, not a big problem for a fit person. Then it's just the walk on the top along a thick, white, dashed line that marks the highest points. Recesses made by lightning bolts are Uluru's scars. They look a bit like moon craters on some of those NASA close-ups.

On my way down, I meet panting people who hold on to the chain.

"How's it going?"

"Good. How's it going?"

"Is it far to the end?" they ask.

"Naaa, it's just this steep part, then it's all right."

"Good on you, mate," is their reply.

A guide, looking like a personal trainer, encourages his student: "Come on! Don't give up! You can do it!"

She hardly catches her breath as she dangles on the chain. "No I can't, I can't."

As soon as I get down, I realise that I left my hat near the top when I sat down to enjoy the view. I need it in this sun. I have to go up. Again. Quickly.

"How's it going?" the same people ask me on the way down.

"Good. How's it going," I reply.

"Is it far to the end?"

"Naaa, it's just that steep part, then it's all right."

They give us a suspicious look like someone who goes through a *déjà vu*: "Good on you, mate. Good on you, mate."

It's a shame we don't get a chance to talk to the real Aboriginal people. They are tucked away in their communities in a permit-only area, far from this place, in parts of the country governed by a combination of Australian law and their customary law. It can be a perfectly orderly community or one with a crime rate fifty times higher than average. The government is somehow trying to tackle this, but it's not something it likes to trumpet to the world. It's still an open wound, covered with a few dishevelled, loose, detached band-aids.

Apparently the first white man to see both Uluru and Kata Tjuta was English immigrant and adventurer Ernest Giles, who explored the area in 1872. There was no naming convention for newly discovered landmarks and the best bet was to choose the name of your boss, sponsor, some kind of royalty or—if you wanted to immortalise it with your name—you only needed one thing—never to return. Giles did return and so he was out of luck for the name. His friend Alfred Gibson however was a 'lucky' bastard. The whole desert bears his name in memoriam. He went missing on one of Giles' expeditions.

These were real explorers, members of the toughest trade; not like us, sissies loaded with conveniences of modern life. Giles only saw Uluru from a distance and didn't have much time to play with names. But he did have a few ideas, like those of his Anglo-German patrons like Sir Ferdinand Jacob Heinrich von Müller. A year later, his rival William Gosse came across the rock and this time didn't hesitate to name it after his employer, South Australian Premier Sir Henry Ayers. Uluru—the name—was first heard only around 1903, "What? Uluru? What a mouthful! It will never catch on!" The Aborigines had to wait ninety years for it to become the official name. It should be read with the underlined r, the so-called retroflex approximant consonant, like letter 'r' pronounced in Texan drawl. But it's rarely used in writing.

Uluru needs to be looked at from many angles. It's different and magnificent from each and every one of them.

39
Sexy Walls: Kata Tju_ta and Kings Canyon

Kata Tju_ta means "many heads" in the local lingo and is also called the Olgas. There are about thirty-six of them, or so, but they are not for trekking. The seven-point-five-kilometre Valley of the Winds[36] has got it all and more, including a very distinctive pattern on one of its walls that, believe it or not, officially doesn't exist. A beautiful piece of natural art could be called Ladies' Privates Rock or Rocky Open Legs.

While Uluru is more or less a smooth monolith, Kata Tjuta has more of a wrinkled rock surface, shapes that sometimes appear to be glued together. The sun on the Walpa Gorge Walk—probably the most popular walk by most visitors because it's closest to the car park—is making those shapes unbelievably vivid, especially one hour or so before the sunset.

Speaking of sunset, it's time to get going. Yulara is fifty kilometres away and Curtin Springs, the next free official spot to stay overnight, is eighty-six kilometres.

Yulara means 'howl' in the local Aboriginal language, probably from dingoes and possibly from tourists reacting to the exorbitant prices of everything you can buy in this little kitsch town. About the only thing that's cheaper here is petrol, so we're in a hurry to get some. It's getting dark, and darkness can mean trouble. With enough bad luck, a well-built kangaroo can turn the car into a worthless piece of junk. Just as the petrol station is round the corner, a siren sounds. Police cars are different in every state and and this one looks more like a fire brigade. He gives us the ultimate farewell souvenir—now an integral part of Australian folklore—a forty kilometre per hour speeding ticket. If you don't get at least one on your travels, you're a lucky bastard. You'd better start playing Powerball.

Now only one third of the puzzle remains: Kings Canyon. The next day we set off from Curtin Springs at 9.30am: we'll be walking its rim in the early afternoon. The drive to Watarrka National

Park took longer than expected. The canyon rocks are very different from Uluru and Kata Tjuta—a bit like little rock beehives. The walls are really steep and it is a long, long way down with no railing at the top. If you slip and fall, you are in Eden, both physically and metaphorically. That's the name of the natural oasis at the bottom, with crystal clear streams, lush greenery and trees, and lots and lots of birds. There had already been a few tourists who had taken the shortcut—a free fall—from Kestrel Falls. We choose the longer route, the walking track to the Lost City and then back to the top. The Kings Canyon Rim Walk is six kilometres long.

40
Coroner on Vacation

Pitching our tent at the Mount Ebenezer Roadhouse, we notice a jolly fellow sitting by the fire. Gary is about fifty and from Melbourne. His young wife died a few years ago. Cancer. He's been working like mad ever since and this is his first holiday in ages. He is articulate, bright and funny. He is a coroner.

Gentle music is coming out of his huge 4x4 with tractor-like wheels. The radio has some issues because occasionally it goes scratchy, and each time, without ever going off his subject, Gary brings it back to life with a mighty punch on the caravan wall. He's taken long service leave and travels like he used to, because this way it feels as if his wife was still with him. He speaks to her when driving and she replies to him, just like that. But then he cheers up, "They owe me. I've been working for them for all those years. I need a break! You wouldn't believe what kind of cases I get. You know what happened to me recently? I have this junkie on the table, a homeless guy. I couldn't believe my eyes. His singlet was the same colour as his skin. No, no. It was part of his skin. You couldn't scrape it off. It was like, like, his own body. Those people! And that's why I love scaring my niece shitless, 'TAKE DRUGS! They will haul you on my desk and dissect you down to the finest detail, to the smallest, tiniest particle. I will have you chopped up, just remember that, you little brat, if you ever, EVER try any drugs!' Or another champ! He had a whole bottle of Coca Cola firmly shoved up his anal canal. How was it even physically possible? Un-fucking-believable!"

A few more morbid cases follow from his long forensic experience until we talk about famous stories, finally bumping into a true classic.

"Yeah," he sighs. "The dingo. I am telling you. She bloody well did it."

41
Busting Dingo

On 17 September 1980, a two-month-old Azaria disappeared from her parents' tent, and despite an exhausting search operation of three hundred plus volunteers, the baby was never found. A week later, her bloodstained clothes and nappies were found. When police asked the parents Michael and Lindy Chamberlain what had happened to their child, the parents gave them a grim answer: it was taken by a dingo. The case was forwarded to the forensic investigator, the blood analysis seemed to reveal Azaria's blood on the back seat of their Holden, and that was the main corpus delicti. The suggestion was that the mother could have killed her with a knife. Nevertheless, there were lots of dingoes spotted around the campground that night and witnesses had heard a crying baby and believed the parents.

They started to shoot dingoes in the vicinity of the Rock in an attempt to find human remains in their stomachs. They even tried to experiment what dogs might do to a chunk of meat wrapped up in baby sleepers. A media circus began feeding millions of people every day with speculations. Tip-offs of all kinds were coming in, about the parents being religious fanatics; she was a witch because she was only dressing in black; it was done by their son who they were now covering for, and so on and so forth.

A year and a month later, almost to the day, police searched the Chamberlain's home and seized about three hundred objects, including the car, which gradually led to a murder charge. The trial was all about what little evidence the prosecution had found. There was little proof against her, but even less against the dingo. The jury finally decided she was guilty and the court sentenced the then pregnant Lindy to life in prison. She appealed this within a year but with no success. New facts were coming to light, most importantly one overturning the hypothesis about blood in the car; there were groups and campaigns lobbying for her release, but all in vain. And that seems like a plain ending to an immensely sad story, but that's only about half of it. Sheer chance took care of the rest. An English backpacker, David Brett, arrived on the sacred Rock to untangle the case once and for all.

In 1986, he decided to climb the Rock in darkness and alone. He went too close to the edge and gravity sent him crashing down hundreds of metres to the earth, falling to his death. Eight days later, when his body was finally found, around an area with a large number of dingo lairs, they chanced on a piece of clothing that turned out to be Azaria's jacket. New speculations saw that the case was finally reopened. In about two years, the parents were acquitted and released but the public opinion was still split and media still hungry. Only there was not so much to feed on any more.

In 2004, a retiree claimed that in 1980 he had shot a dingo with a dead infant in his mouth. He only wanted to testify after twenty-four years or so because he had shot the dog illegally and was afraid of the penalties. Police wrote the details down and made another record in their big database of loonies. Only in 2012, thirty-two years after the tragedy, a coroner pronounced a final ruling on Azaria's death: she was killed by a wild dingo.

The sobbing mother's cry at her first interview has turned into an Australian iconic phrase. "A dingo's got my baby!" That's what's left of the famous case.

"But I am telling you," says Gary, "she bloody well did it."

42
Where Mad Max Drove: Breakaways

Kulgera, a small settlement with a petrol station, is about a two-hour drive from Mount Ebenezer. It's noon when we cross the border to South Australia. Cadney Homestead Roadhouse is a little bit further south, and that's where we meet Alex for the second time. He's fixing his super-thin road bike tyre. Another puncture. He has a friend now, a sixty-year-old Japanese guy, Sumio, also on a trip through the centre. The weather change has made itself felt on the cyclists' faces.

Sumio is a big fan of Go Game, a very old Chinese board game, possibly the oldest board game in the world. There are whole online tournaments. Sumio explains. "Unlike chess, the board is bigger, the rules seem very simple, with only white and black stones, but strategically the game is very complex. It's all about gaining more territory, while playing on multiple parts of the board at the same time."

Strange landscape of Breakaways, SA[37]

We head south in the morning. About thirty-two kilometres before Coober Pedy, a tiny left turn leads to the Breakaways, a separate mountain range that, as the name suggests, broke off from the larger Stuart Range. This didn't happen last week, but around the time the dinosaurs disappeared from the Earth's surface. It was under the sea then. After eleven kilometres of good dirt road, a very strange landscape opens up. What was once the seabed many millions of years ago has become a unique spectacle: a landscape without any regularity or rule, which is why filmmakers love it so much, especially the creators of Mad Max.

Going further would take us to the dog fence that protects pasturelands of the south from the wild dingoes in the north. It's 5,300 kilometres long.

By the way, our journey is about in the middle now: the fortieth day on the road and there are six and a half thousand more kilometres to go. That's shortly before Coober Pedy, one of the most enigmatic places in Australia. What's there can't be found anywhere else.

VI. White Bloke Down a Pit

43
Opal Land: the Ingenuity of Coober Pedy

The name evokes thousands of holes, pits and shafts, dug out for miles and miles far beyond the town. Even before entering the place itself, we can't help thinking, we're in some kind of weird giant industrial zone, searched through over and over again by heavy machinery, ending as one superbig ant heap.

It's windy and cold. It's not that hot Australia that one sees on postcards. A big nicely coloured dumper truck on hoisted legs marks a symbolic entrance to the town[38], suggesting this will be a home to heavy duty. Warning signs are everywhere. "Don't run", "Don't walk backwards", "Beware, deep shafts", "Unmarked holes", "Blasting", "Penalty for unauthorised entry to mining claims"[39]. There were a good few who ended stuck with their heads down. The town itself makes quite a good dusty impression: rough but pleasant. The main paved road branches off to unpaved roads, where we dodge piles of debris that are actually houses. They call them dugouts and they can be anything from people's homes to churches—Catholic, Orthodox, Serbian, Greek, and even a dugout camping ground. All rugged, covered in dust, and very original.

Warning signs shortly before Coober Pedy, SA

And then there are the opals. That's how it all started.

The beginning of the twentieth century was not particularly kind to many immigrants. People were chasing money wherever they could, and when they didn't have any, they could simply starve. Real poverty without any cushions. In 1915, a four-member expedition set out to explore the outback on camels. They were there to look for riches of the land. Their main problem was water. There wasn't enough of it anywhere and all explorers were depending on finding it, otherwise they'd have to head back. This group was no exception. The heat and drought were unbearable. The temperature was high, above forty. Looking for water took an excessive amount of time and they only had enough for a few more days. The fifteen-year old Bill Hutchinson was assigned to look after the campsite in the morning, when three older members set out to find some water. On their return, the fire was out and Bill had disappeared.

"Where the hell is he?" thought his father.

Anger was soon replaced by worry, and when it got dark the chances of finding him quickly dwindled. They put more wood in the fire and hoped he would see it and find his way back.

"Where have you been? Didn't I tell you to look after the camp?" his father shouted as Bill suddenly appeared.

"Look!" says Bill.

"You could have died out there—!"

But Bill didn't listen. He'd found water and this strange little stone called an opal, which at first he thought was some desert rubbish. After the news spread around Adelaide, a new kind of fever broke out. More and more people came to dig. Deeper and deeper.

And the natives, thinking that something wasn't quite right with these white men, must have shaken their heads in disbelief and said: "Kupa piti". "Kupa piti."

The white bloke is sitting in a hole! The white bloke in a ditch.

That's how the town is said to have got its modern name: Coober Pedy.

The business was good until the Great Depression almost wiped it out in 1931, turning the place into a ghost town.

Everybody seems to have something to do with opals here. At a petrol station, hotel or a museum, everything shines in opal.

"Buying opal", "Opal dealer", "Opal Inn", "Opal displays", "Opal shop", "Opal gallery", "Opal cutter", opal this, opal that. As for the wholesale, the Chinese are said to be doing well selling it to their enormous market, increasingly hungry for luxury items. The local retail is very diverse.

Beautifully rough: Coober Pedy from a hotel roof and a spaceship left behind by film-makers,[40] SA

Small sandpits set up in front of many shops invite people to noodle: rake for traces of common opals, or potch, which is opal without much colour or worth.

We are in a shop owned by a German family who has been in the area for a long time. There are black and white pictures all around the walls, showing their humble beginnings, he and his wife sitting in their own dugout living room. He arrived in Australia with nothing, and from a city he came to the end of the world here to spend years by digging in the ground. He's worked his way up. At the moment he is at a trade fair somewhere in Germany, doing business selling opals.

The nicer potch stones are sold as souvenirs for small amounts, because the more colour, the more dollars. A Croatian shop assistant has been here a long time too.

"There are people from everywhere. Any nationality," she says.

In a cosy restaurant down the street later that afternoon, we meet an exceptionally nice lady and her son. Though Bronia has been here for many years, even her son Bobby still speaks a charming variant of Czech.

"I had a lot of aunties and uncles over there in Czechoslovakia, you know, but they all pissed away—" he says after some conversation.

"*Passed away*, you mean?", we offer.

"Oh, *passed away*, of course, *DIED*!" he says with a cheeky grin. "Sorry, I am confusing the two."

Bronia comes from Moravia and used to be good at car racing. But she was not in love with the regime and so she and her Slovakian husband chose to flee. Then Bobby was born as a true Czecho-Slovakian Australian who used both languages with his parents until he found English was easier. Her husband passed away a few years ago and she lives with Peter, her second partner.

Bobby jokes that most of the time he swaps the words *kostel* (church) for *postel* (bed) and *žaludek* (stomach) for *žalud* (glans penis), because they are kind of similar. Otherwise he speaks without any major issues.

They have a beautifully equipped kitchen and we suggest that we cook something traditional for them they would know, like goulash stew. Okay, deal. We do a round trip of the town first, seeing an underground opal mine on the way, plus a few more opal shops; and with ingredients, we march back in, ready for some action. The kitchen has everything we need. There are loads of people coming and going: here is a guy as big as a mountain, in a boiler suit covered by at least a millimetre layer of dust, there are others who frequently come and go like in an open space office, there is a young blonde who whispers something in Bobby's ear, gives him a gentle hug and then disappears.

"I'll be back in twenty. Just need to give somebody a ride," says

Bobby.

Bronia's boyfriend Bobby works as a relief teacher at the local public school. But he is also a part-time treasure hunter. After work, he spends hours outside the town noodling.

The dinner is ready but it's still early. He asks me to go to school with him to do a little job. We'll be back in twenty minutes. He greets everybody as we drive along. I figure he must have been here for a long time.

He needs to cut some planks for a new shelf and the school has a perfect workshop. In Coober Pedy, practical skills are simply crucial. "Fix your car? No problem. How much did they ask for the filter? Noooo! You must be kidding. Well, mate, they ripped you off. I would have done it for you for free in five minutes. Remember, never look like a tourist or they will eat you alive."

44
Indigenous Versus Conventional: Take III

When Peter takes me through the town, he spots a local Aboriginal crossing the street. He wears a thick loose-fitting coat, a worn knitted hat, and a long scarf that is partly covering his face. It's cold, quite cold now. He carries a bottle in his hand and is staggering a bit on the dirty roadside. He gets Peter's attention.

"Do you know how old this guy is?" he asks.

I turn my head to have one more glimpse.

"Not sure. Sixty?"

"This one is around forty, I know him. He's only going to live a few more years," he adds after a moment. "It's sad how they live," he continues. "They only eat canned food, white bread, no vegetables. They are malnourished, they don't have enough vitamins, basic nutrients. They end up with diabetes or heart condition. And that's not counting the booze. They live seventeen years shorter in average. Those who live to fifty-five can consider themselves lucky."

Shortly before getting to the school, Peter meets his colleague, a female teacher. A short exchange and he drives on. "Nice girl, but she needs better English to be a teacher. The young ones speak too colloquially and pass the blabber to kids."

We get out of the car. The school workshop is so state–of-the–art it could as well be a small factory. There are all kinds of machines, from simple table drill presses to quite advanced lathes.

I can't help returning to the previous topic and while he clamps his wooden planks, between cutting sounds of the circular saw, I listen to what he has to say.

"The Aboriginal way of life is actually 'communism' in its purest form. Property is common to the group—they have a different concept of ownership. Any competition is regarded as undesirable. That's simply their way to survive. Once somebody is sticking out from the crowd, that's unwanted behaviour and they are reprimanded, or even excluded from the rest. It makes sense to them but it's hard for us to understand. You have to turn everything you think about possessions upside down. There was this huge clash. Non-materialistic culture and highly materialistic culture went head to head and guess who won. I was always asking myself why the Aboriginal children never wanted to make anything in practical workshops. Then I found out that anything they would make at school would automatically be confiscated at home. Parents or uncles, it doesn't matter. The elders have even more say than the parents. They can punish the kids. Let's say we make a wooden chair from those planks, the boy brings it home and they chop it up and burn it as fuel for communal warmth. Or anything else. They will grab it from him the moment they see it. So why would a child want to make something at school? And they have a different sense of time. They were never obsessed with it. It's like time doesn't exist for them. They show up at school for two days and then disappear for a week. That's the stuff that makes the whites not want to send their kids to the same school. It's not racism. And the amount of money they spend on booze, there's none left to feed the kids. They are one big family, the whole community of members. Hygiene can be a problem. What if I told you that some of them confused the toilet bowl with the sink? Sometimes ten or more live in one house, somebody dies there and they all move out, never to live there again. All this housing money from the government has gone out the window."

"How about the stolen generation?" I interrupt.

"Let's face reality here, look at the practical side. As sad as it was, they were the first well-educated generation of Aborigines that could wash, tidy up, and find a job. My point is we're here to stay. We're not going anywhere now, are we? We're one. So they had better get used to it because now they can't walk it alone any more."

45
Welcome and Piss Off: On How to Find and Not to Lose

We're back at the restaurant.

"What is that shit?" asks the spooky hulk in the boiler suit, who has seen the stew with dumplings while passing the kitchen. He pulls a yucky face. "Gimme a meat pie," then he's gone.

After the dinner, it's time for some drinks and we move to the local pub. Peter and Bronia go home. They invite us later to their dugout house. We sit with Bobby and Amy, his fiancée.

"Do you know why there is so much sex in Coober Pedy?" says Bobby in a bored voice.

"No."

"Beaches everywhere but no water."

Sex on the Beach is Midori, plus vodka, plus Bacardi, plus Bailey's. There is the Squashed Frog: Midori, Advocaat Liqueur, plus a bit of Grenadine syrup with raspberry juice. And the Centipede. Kahlua, Bailey's, Grenadine syrup.

"Coober is not very safe," he goes on. "There used to be about thirty people in my class, now there's only about half of them. The rest went nuts. Like, some of them surfed—did you know you can surf here? You just get an old loose car bonnet and tow it behind your car for blokes to jump on. Full throttle. Add a bit of gambling in your spare time, drugs, and you're screwed. What else can you do here? Not many girls. The nearest, like, normal township is Adelaide, 850 kilometres away. I'm going there in five days. You can come with me."

Dugout church in Coober Pedy, SA[41]

The subject changes to opals. "If you grow up here, you develop an eye for it. It's never just a clean, shiny stone lying on the ground, waiting for you. You see a tiny tip that looks almost exactly like all the rocks around it, dirty and grey. Often it's not even a stone. It's a mussel. But they are worth more. You can find thousands of dollars like that. I once found one that's worth sixteen thousand. Wait a minute!"

Before we say anything he hops into his car and disappears.

We look around. The pub is chock-a-block, which means full to the last seat. The party at the next table is having a heated bogan debate.

"*—yooooooouu're a fucking legend mate, aren't ya?*" one of them exclaims.

"*Mate, you have noooo idea, have ya? HAVE YA? NO—FUCK-ING—IDEA, moron!*" the other retorts, then starts to explain something in language too fast for us to understand. But not for long.

"FUCK OFF!" The first one cuts in, as if not wanting to listen any more. Then they all burst into a long, uncontrollable fit of laughter.

Bobby is back in ten minutes. The opal looks exactly like a mussel, except it's all blue with flickering colours. So we truly are on the seabed.

"Once you find an opal, you think you'll find it again. And so you search and search. It's like a slot machine. Like gambling. I knew a guy who found three hundred thousand worth of opals. In six months he didn't have enough money to change his tyre."

The pub starts to pulsate. Young and not so young, all start to sing and dance.

We're staying in the underground camp tonight but we've no idea how to get there.

To us, all the rubble piles outside look exactly the same.

"I'll get you there. Don't you worry," shouts Bobby.

Bobby's phone rings. We're going to Peter's.*

Peter's dugout is like an underground castle. It's got at least five large rooms and he says he's going to dig out more when he runs out of space.

"This place is for the strong. Wimps won't last. You have to show your muscle sometimes. A neighbour of mine used to tip rubbish next to my ventilation shaft, making compost. Terrible pong was coming in the house with every blast of wind. Rotten stuff.

"I asked him all the time, nice and polite, begging him to remove it. Na! He didn't care. So I took a dead bird and hung it down his shaft. In a few days the stink disappeared. He got the message.

"Or look at people who noodle on others' lots. You spend thousands for preparation, and then some lout from a city somewhere touches down on your sandpit to sponge off your work." He speaks about leases further afield; only potch is found in the town now.

"They're risking their own arse, I'm telling you. The first shot is in the air. From time to time, somebody gets clubbed or shot. But that's the insiders. Outside tourists, like you, who behave, can take it easy. If you want to live here, you need to earn respect. And to pay respect."

We're trying his home-made cognacs and whiskeys. They are very good, and he explains the process. If they were poured from an original bottle, we wouldn't know the difference. Peter is incredibly versatile. One minute he can talk about bootlegging, then change to the innards of a car engine, and just few minutes later he shows he is also well versed in the greatest classical music composers of the nineteenth century.

At half past twelve, Bobby's phone rings again. Amy has cut her finger badly when opening a fruit can. She is as pale as a ghost when we arrive, but luckily, an ambulance is not necessary.

Bobby sits slumped on a chair, tired. We all are.

"Forget the underground camp. Just stay in my house," he says finally, two minutes before falling asleep.

*

Peter's noodling machinery is on the other side of the town and is in full swing the next day. He gave us directions on how to get there, but they're not clear. Once past the town, it's easy to get lost[42]. Mounds of dirt and more mounds of dirt, one next to another, for kilometres without an end. Peter has an excavator he uses to scoop large chunks of earth and then load onto a conveyor belt—another machine—where he separates rocks from better pieces like potch, gypsum and hopefully opal. The rest of the dirt is spewed out of the machine, making another big mound next to it.

Excavator loads dirt onto a conveyor belt ...

Anything but dirt stands out on the belt like shiny spots in a dark room, where he spends some time and then emerges with a bucketful of carefully selected rubbish. Most of it, like the potch, is completely worthless, other stuff like gypsum, you'd need a few tonnes to make any money. He throws it in anyway. Just in case. He will examine it during the day or later at home. He does a few cycles like this and then prescribes himself a break.

... then it's sifted in the dark room

"See, this is my lot. You have to have a permit before you start to … oh shit—!" He has just remembered something and quickly leaves. I am not sure whether to follow him or wait. He stands by one of the marking posts and overwrites something with a permanent marker and a piece of rag. "I forgot it expired yesterday."

Sifting machinery[43] in full swing

"There! You see, it's all about trying. There are days and days when you find bugger-all but then, in a single stroke of luck, you can find a few thousand dollars. The last one I found was a fossil. The best you can do then is to hide it in a good safe and keep your mouth shut until you sell it. You're not going to put on public display in a local pub."

Whoops.

Alex and Sumio stand next to their bikes by the Orthodox Church dugout in Coober Pedy. Each time we see them, we plunge into a combination of pity and admiration of their strong will.

Another rest place is Bon Bon, about 200 kilometres south. It's quite cold now but one of my legs starts swelling—a delayed tropical skin rash. It's only going to be sorted by a doctor in Melbourne. Bon Bon on the Stuart Highway is good for having a rest and not much more. It's only a dot in the midst of barren land. It's not far from the road, and the dry tree limbs and roots will do to make a fire. A hot meal saves the day. We realise that somewhere around the Red Centre we lost warm nights. The difference in temperature at day and night is significant now.

Two headlights are coming near from the other direction. Backpackers going north. They put up their tent and join us at the fireplace, making *damper*, simple bread from self-rising flour and water baked in the fire ash or on a stick. We can tell them what's ahead of them and they can tell us what awaits us in the opposite direction.

46
Firecracker Town: Woomera

All the dried-up Lake Hart can offer is a car wreck of a small van and thousands of annoying flies. And a perfect backdrop for a picture. Its silver, salty bed shows marks of what once used to be a jetty, a long row of wooden dots gnawed by time and weather.

Woomera, not far from here, is an interesting end to the South Australian opal territory.

It is a purpose-built town, used to be closed to the public, and was used as a military base for soldiers and scientists working on rocket programs. From the air it would look like a small suburb in the middle of a desert. It was designed during the Cold War to test long-range ballistic missiles. It's a gate to "nowhere". To add insult to injury, the governments in the fifties used this and other Aboriginal lands for nuclear programs, even having a few testing blasts in places like Maralinga and Emu.

Right after the last street, thousands of kilometres of barren land starts and the ramp that used to fire the rockets got its name from Aboriginal spear-thrower: Woomera. There are few people now, mainly employees of the local museum. It nostalgically reminds of those pompous times.

Rocket park in Woomera,[44] SA

Today's administration is more secretive. If there is a research station somewhere, it will be well hidden from public sight, thousands of kilometres even from here.

In the nineties, Woomera found a new use as a refugee detention centre. During riots in the year 2000, about five hundred refugees took it to the streets, protests were surpressed, and later the whole facility was moved somewhere else.

An older Australian told me the other day that he never knew what side of the road a car would come from. The American Jeeps didn't bother driving on the left side, sometimes going on the left, sometimes on the right, depending on their mood. It used to be a government domain and probably still is. The town is just waiting for a new opportunity.

VII. Port Augusta to Melbourne

47

Tough Luck Mountains: Flinders Ranges

Port Augusta is where the soul of one Australia more or less ends and another one begins: more civilised, slightly more inhabited and coastal. Up until now, the itinerary was relatively simple. One way: south. Now this road will fork out into dozens of options.

The outback is actually one huge elevation without mountains—a dry plateau, positioned moderately above sea level with rather unfriendly winds steadily blowing across it. Shortly before Port Augusta,[45] this plateau gives way to a gradual descent to the coast. We're going down as if from hills which are not there. A place called Lake Hart is the beginning of one of the largest drainage basins in the world: Lake Eyre. It is also the only place in Australia that is actually below sea level. If the climate so desires, the water capacity of the area is larger than a few European countries combined, but most of the time it's dry.

Dried up Lake Hart: Part of Lake Eyre basin,[46] SA

Port Augusta is still a small town—a foray into Adelaide, which in itself is not too large. City life in the true sense is still far away. One knows that from looking at the cars. The shiny city darlings are nowhere to be seen yet, and there are only the more robust breed of mainly four-wheel drives or their shabby-looking two-wheel cousins like ours, with remnants of red dust over their number plates. Large trucks pass us in both directions, even one carrying a whole house like a giant "snail" with two little flashing car "ants", one in front and the second in rear, holding the Oversize sign. We have to stop and make way. Not far from here to the north-west and on our left, there are some of the most extraordinary landscapes of Australia, a range that might just as well be tagged the "tough luck" mountains—the Flinders Ranges, also known as Ikara.

Road to Ikara-Flinders Ranges, SA

Matthew Flinders was actually the guy who most vigorously advocated "Australia" for its official name, but his legacy is somehow lost among the accomplishments of his more famous contemporaries. He spent some six years in prison on Mauritius, where he arrived not knowing that France was at war with England, he was wrecked on reefs in Queensland once when sailing back home to England; while he survived, he lost all his possessions including his precious diaries. He died at only forty years old. Yet he managed to circumnavigate Australia and also document it on maps.

As far as fate is concerned, 'his' Ranges are—a little bit like himself. They were largely settled by pioneers from northern Europe, mainly country people and farmers. The scenario was repeated many times. Each year at Christmas, the humble families would sit around their tables in quiet obedience, praying to God for rain, to at last irrigate their thirsty land, feed their cows, bring better crops, and generally improve their livelihoods. They prayed in their first year. Nothing. They prayed in their second year. Nothing again. They were praying for a few more years. And still nothing. And then the rain came. It came and stayed for long enough time to flood the whole area and ruin everything they had built in all those years.

Ruins left behind by settlers in Ikara-Flinders Ranges, SA

There was even a decent rail track linking the local towns; steam trains today known as Pichi Richi that give a good taste of what it looked like in those times.

The long, straight drive into the Flinders Ranges is like stepping back in time. There are many empty stone house foundations where families once lived, all against the backdrop of the magnificent hills. Its original name, Ikara remembers much more and goes thousands of years into the past. A touch of magic.

One of such eerie places is Wilpena Pound[47]—a hill formation that from high above looks like a meteor crater, but is actually an ancient seabed. It used to be called *Adnyamathanha* by the Aborigines, meaning "meeting place". Later the farmers wanted to take advantage of it as a natural enclosure for cattle herds, but Mother Nature thought better of it. With one extreme to another, it drove them away with no remorse. And so they left their homes behind. We are lucky they didn't build them with today's fibro building standards. There would be nothing left. Frost forms on our tent in the morning, combining perfectly with the rising sun. The campground is comfortable, even with music in the toilets. We're hiking on St Mary Peak—or Ngarri Mudlanha[48]—the highest peak of Flinders Ranges at 1,171 metres above sea level.

Wilpena Pound "crater", SA: View from St Mary Peak

Not much, you might say, but it's a five-hour, full-attention walk. Parts of the 'crater' can be seen from above, and the top is covered with large slabs of rock with cliffs and steep falls. A black currawong bird greets us with its characteristic ominous call. Throw a piece of bread into the abyss and it will know exactly where it fell, such is the sharpness of its vision.

St Mary Peak/Ngarri Mudlanha, SA: 1,171 m ASL

When driving back, this picturesque scenery ends near Port Augusta.

Here somewhere the more inhabited Australia begins, a different chapter as it were, although it is not nearly as populous as we initially expect and it changes slowly and gradually.

48
Adelaide in a Nutshell

The world's biggest rocking horse, in Gumeracha on the northeast slopes of Adelaide, is a tall structure in front of a toy factory and another one of the Australian 'biggies collection'. The smell of coffee and freshly worked wood is just too irresistible.

Big Rocking Horse in Gumeracha, SA[49]

The road from Port Augusta to Adelaide goes through a rolling landscape, and we're here at a time when everything is lushly green among the farmhouses, vineyards and fields.

Adelaide is the only Australian city that predominantly used sandstone and brick as building materials because wood was in short supply. The tram to Glenelg, the beach part, feels a bit like Vienna.

South Australia is the driest state, the government is its largest employer, and there are only about one and a half million people. Only about ten percent of people live outside the capital.

For now we don't need to know more because we're only in transit here.

This time a transit to prehistoric times.

49
Fifty Thousand Years Ago: Naracoorte

The South Australian town of Naracoorte is surrounded by agricultural land, and at first sight there seems to be nothing interesting here[50]. Victoria is around the corner, but because they discovered something amazingly weird in this place, something that can only be seen here, it's not the right time to cross the border yet.

Diprotodon optatum was one of the largest marsupials that ever lived on the planet. It was a wombat-beast as big as grizzly, but instead of tearing its victim apart with sharp teeth, it would rather stash it in its giant pouch and chew on it later. A giant hamster. On close examining the size of its jaw, it might comfortably fit a person with backpack and a camera on a tripod.

The giant wombat: Naracoorte Caves National Park

Procoptodon goliah, for a change, was a gigantic kangaroo. It was about two to three metres tall and it weighed about two hundred kilos. I don't want to think what that mass could do to a car in a head-on collision. It is well known, however, that very strange creatures used to live in this part of South Australia, and this was, in eternity terms, not so long ago: only some fifty thousand years back. Marsupial lions with terrible, large tusks, huge koalas, at least twenty kangaroo types of scary proportions, and many other rather unpronounceable species.

Their demise, interestingly enough, coincides with the first traces of humans on the continent. They probably didn't leave voluntarily. First Australians are said to have helped them on their way out, with their systematic killing and burning their food.

There are many caves in Australia, but this particular one, with a museum at its front, is heritage-listed. Bats live here too: not the much-hated macrochiroptera, which feed on fruit, but the microchiroptera, which use ultrasound to navigate. They live in total darkness. Tourists regularly visit them with their thermal auras, sending thousands of micro-particles of sweat, cheap clothes, street dust and breath vapours into the cave walls. As an American tourist once jokingly told me, "If the cave walls are not green enough, the cave is not making enough money". But this cave seems to be managed responsibly. There's no light inside because there are tiny insects that the bats depend on. If the insects die, so do the bats.

"Whoops," whispers someone in the crowd. "We used to camp and play our guitars here when we were young."

Naracoorte is not just a piece of history. Good wines are produced here, although not as famous as the neighbouring Barossa Valley. Vineyards of known brands are glimmering on the side of the narrow road as we go along. There are massive trees along that road. At one of them, a sign is attached about a young backpacker girl who was killed here in a car accident. She was driving to work and had a head-on collision with a truck. We're heading to a farm, where we will stay with the people we met in Ormiston Gorge.

Ben and Heather have a farm with two thousand sheep. Sometimes they have to move them to their other property, ten kilometres from the house. It takes all day to move the flock. It's a big open area with lots of stumps. A large black magpie squawks nearby with a vicious sound. A hyena bird, they say. When a sheep has to give birth and falls to the ground, it can peck out her eyes. Another animal drama happens later that day. The sheep are being counted in their enclosures when one of them freaks out and breaks her leg on the metal fence. This is tantamount to suicide, as it has to be slaughtered immediately. It must have known where it was going: to the nearby abattoir that afternoon. But the farmer doesn't like killing his own sheep, that is obvious.

His sheepdog is a skilled champion. He puts on a real show, jumping on the sheep's backs and knowing exactly which way to go, left or right, at the slightest change in his master's voice.

The next day we cross the border into Victoria and camp that night on Mount Arapiles. A perfectly quiet spot, good for a rest by the fire, and home to a traditional climbing community. The tiny dots on the rocky hills opposite our tent are people climbing the local rocky walls. Although we don't know it yet, this is a nice prelude to something even more fascinating: The Grampians.

50
All Seasons in One Day: Grampians

Only a few days ago, I thought that nothing could be as remote as the outback. I didn't know we would drive to a place called Chimney Pots. It's complete solitude. The Grampians is a crazy mountain range, not only in weather patterns, but also in the character of its tracks.

But first we're off to Stawell, our first gate into the National Park. We're staying with our friends Jim and Sarah. They have a nice little house, a teenage daughter who doesn't reply to a greeting and an old dog who haphazardly walks through rooms, bumps into furniture and regularly marches into their fireplace. And in between his barking episodes, Jim asks if we have ever heard of a 'Nerve Test'. No, we haven't. Apparently there is a place in the park - a ledge - that can really test your nerves, he says. The problem is, we can't find it on the maps.

"Don't worry. You'll see it, it's a well-known place". So the next day we head for Halls Gap, the real gate to the park.

Hail in Silent Street: Grampians/Gariwerd

The creek water on the *Wonderland Walk*, has a colour of beer and climbs from the *Grand Canyon*[51]. The subsequent trail leads through a little forest to a narrow path between two rock walls. There are ladders and the gully is called *Silent Street*. It was nice and sunny down at the car park, but hail fell on our heads and quickly turned to snowflakes. It's the first time we've seen snow in Australia and it's quite a surprise. These are Grampians—also known as Gariwerd—where all seasons can come together in one day.

The stony path is very slippery, and a fast-moving fog greets us at the top. By the time we finally reach the spot called the Pinnacle, a snowstorm is raging around.

The guy at the information centre didn't want to tell us where the Nerve Test was. He was all shilly-shally before admitting "it was not advertised any more". It's actually just a few hundred metres from the Pinnacle,

Soaking wet we walk through the Grampians Gardens, back to the Wonderland car park and then back to Stawell, to a nice fireplace where the poor old dog continues his danse macabre. He must have burned his snout at least a hundred times by now.

"Do you know the Hollow Mountain?" Jim starts again. And he hands me a book where a track called "Mount Stapylton to Hollow Mountain" is dubbed the most beautiful track in Australia.

The book is from the 80s, an ordinary book, no pictures. Boring. Modern tourist guides are beautiful, have coloured pictures and usually make tracks look more difficult than they really are. A just in case approach so we automatically just half the estimated walking times because we know they are exaggerated. This book on the other hand says this track is five kilometres long and it takes five hours. Surely, a five-kilometre walking track will not take five hours! What a load of bullshit!

But it will. In fact, it will take more than that.

51
What the Guides Won't Say: The Real Peaks of Grampians

The starting point to Mount Stapylton is on the north-east side of the park. From Stawell it's half-way to Horsham, passing the Giant Koala[52] and turning left to get to Mount Zero Picnic Area[53]. That's our point zero. Most people will pass it because they're too keen on getting to the heart of the park and will never see the best walking track.

Giant Koala, VIC

Mount Stapylton to Hollow Mountain deserves to be called one of the most adrenaline-pumping tracks in Australia. It's mentally and physically challenging and not actively promoted. The weather, as mentioned, can add to the difficulty and catch even the most experienced hikers off guard. Just a few months ago, people got lost in Grampians and it took three days to rescue them. They were still alive but severely hypothermic. These mountains are not high, but very rugged and steep. This trail in particular has many descents where it's easy to fall—and fall far and deep.

The first part to Mount Stapylton is still on our map and is easy.

It goes slightly uphill along a massive rock platform until it reaches a remarkable natural sculpture called Bird Rock, because it looks like a large squatting bird. The track becomes steeper from this point, and after about twenty minutes the surrounding rocks become slightly confusing. Sometimes it's not quite clear where to go. We cling to the trail that goes left and try to get up to where it officially ends: Mount Stapylton.

Bird rock: Mount Stapylton

Wind blows at the top and an interesting view opens up. The 'bird' can be spotted down from the cliff and we are surrounded by chaos of rock formations. They are somehow arranged into three distinct that can be seen on the map—a labyrinth that is quite difficult to find your way through. . The goal is to find an opening in the rock at the other side, an opening that spirals down about five metres through the rock mass and lead back to the car park.

Mount Stapylton to Hollow Mountain, VIC

After five minutes, we're lost. The detailed word description doesn't help. It's all going downhill in all directions, first slowly, then steeper so that we can't see over the horizon how far it actually goes. Putting our rucksacks aside, we spend a good half hour looking for the most plausible route, returning to the same spot several times.

After a great deal of effort and mental strain, we manage to slowly descend a rockslide, not to find an abyss, but a track that leads further on. It's been well hidden the whole time. We try to keep to the rocky path and never descend too far. If we descend too far, it means we are on the wrong path. At one point there are high rock chimneys, but the way forward is hidden again. There is a used carabiner on the ground. It's a popular climbing spot too.

Sometimes we lie down and admire the long steep walls around us to calm down. There are a few places between the ridges where the rock is split by a narrow but very long and deep crack. We have to cross it at the highest point, as there is rarely a less frightening way around.

Suddenly voices come from behind. Two young guys from Melbourne with a slightly better map, but no less surprise on their faces. The next crack is even longer and deeper. It's split open for the whole length of the ridge. It's now more than clear that we're going to have to cross it somewhere and the gap is smallest at the highest point. The fact that it's already afternoon and that heavy clouds are forming over our heads doesn't help. A jump is out of the question. There is nowhere to land. We cross. Slowly and carefully.

Walls of Mount Stapylton

Next is a large natural atrium with a large fallen tree in the middle. We find a couple of ways out, but they are all blind. We're losing precious time again: we didn't take a torch in case it got dark. As if we hadn't made that mistake before.

Only few cracks lead out of the atrium. Managing to get through one of the narrower ones, we're out, on the outside rock surface again. Trying to keep as high on the crest as possible, we get to a place where there is no way forward. The vertical wall of another ridge is opposite, and every direction from where we stand runs steeply down. That's the other side of the track, because now, we're on the other peak called Hollow Mountain. It's time to find the rock opening. There are four of us and we search for about half an hour. Nature was playing a trick because it is on the other side, well hidden from the way we chose.

Hollow Mountain, the Grampians, VIC

Spiralling down to safety after a five hours' walk, we only now get talking to our co-hikers. Where we come from, what we saw, and this place—how it's crazy.

"So, what's your name?" I ask, after introducing myself at last.

"David," says the first one.

"He is David *Lynch*," says the other one with a grin.

"Beautiful. And you have just conquered the *Twin Peaks*. Isn't that kinda cool? Nice to meet you!"

52
Clay and Whales: Great Ocean Road

We say goodbye to Stawell with a look at its gold mine. Heavy trucks with funny flattened cabins disappear into an entrance in the ground that leads kilometres under the surface. They re-emerge from another opening with haul beds full of dirt, tip the load and off they go again. The golden bench we sit on represents the amount of gold the mine has yielded in all its existence. That's it. Just one cuboid shape you can sit on.

Beautiful green landscapes populated by thousands of sheep stretch from here to the coast ending up in the pride landmark of Victoria called the Great Ocean Road. Warrnambool is where we start. We're in time to watch whales. They come every year around September and they show off their huge fins and bellies only a few hundred metres from the shore. When you're patient enough for them to come out of water a bit more, you realise how enormous this animal really is.

The rugged coastline can be fully appreciated from certain points. It's not rocky, but made of very hard clay. Many places are dangerous. Getting up from the water after a fall would be almost impossible.

The London Bridge,[54] about seventy kilometres from Warrnambool, used to be—as its name suggests—a bridge, but in 1990 it collapsed and stranded a couple of lovers on what became an island with no bridge to the other side. Lucky for them, they had already crossed it when it went down. They wouldn't have survived otherwise. In a bit of shock, they were rescued by a helicopter a few hours later. The rumour went around they were extremely lucky cheaters. This coast is also famous for its large number of ship-wrecks, most of them from the nineteenth century, when many of the first settlers died tragically here. After months of gruelling sea voyages, many never walked on the shore. That's why the stretch from Moonlight Head to Port Fairy is called the Shipwreck Coast. About eighty ships perished here.

London Bridge, rough Victorian coast[55]

What's interesting is that some of these ships may have been wrecked well before the 19th century, so they may not necessarily have been English. They may have been Portuguese, but that's just speculation as no evidence has been found. If found, it would rewrite the history books.

The Twelve Apostles[56] are not twelve but rather eight or so. Some of them will collapse and new ones will emerge over time. A long time. In the meantime, the creative name attracts thousands in bus tours. More trivial names were considered, like Sow and Piglets, but the current name did extremely well. It's one of the best known tourist attractions. The winding road along the coast is worth every inch of the way.

It is rather cold in the Cumberland River Holiday Park, seven kilometres from Lorne, but there is a beautifully whispering river not far from our fireplace. Torquay is Great Ocean Road's end station. Wild sea lashes its beaches and is therefore a respected surfing venue. One of its kind in Australia. The "capital of surf", according to the locals.

Big city life is just a stone's throw away. It's Geelong that heralds something even bigger. We clean the car from mud and dust because we're only one step away from Melbourne.

53
Melbourne in a Nutshell

In 1852, a man stepped off the S.S. Great Britain onto a barge on the banks of the Yarra River. He was one of many—an ex-soldier exiled to Britain after two unsuccessful insurgent campaigns in Europe. His native Poland, divided between Austria, Prussia and Russia since 1795, would not appear on the map for more than half a century. In fact, he was not to see his homeland gain independence for the rest of his life.

He was fluent in German and French but was unable to find employment in London for his limited knowledge of English and also his total unwillingness, or rather categorical refusal to shave off his hook moustache, a condition imposed by the English for him to work as a language teacher. Instead, at the age of 52, he and five of his compatriots embarked on a long and dangerous journey to the goldfields of Victoria.

Seweryn Korzelinski lived and worked in Australia for 4 years, and the treasure he brought home was not gold. It was his diary, which miraculously survived four years of incredibly harsh conditions, long and arduous sea voyages, the dust of non-existent rough roads, rainy nights in makeshift shelters, bush raids and fires. His handwritten memoirs, meticulously written and carefully protected, describe in incredible detail what Australia was like in the 1850s—just seventy years after being colonised by the European settlers in an era without the luxuries of modern times. He made many comparisons with Europe, America and Asia, made many interesting geopolitical observations, described in great detail the indigenous population and settlers, clearly distinguishing between those from the Anglo-Saxon world and those from mainland Europe. Although his comments were not always favourable to the British, he held the Crown in the highest regard. He saw Australia through the crucial historical period of the Eureka Stockade, when Australia's system of government was being shaped and its fate, in a sense, sealed. He explained the politics, economics, rules and regulations of the time and even made some predictions.

We spent our first few hours in Melbourne scouring scrap yards for the rear window of our car and trying to find a doctor to treat the tropical infection on my leg. The window was out there somewhere, and for a fair price. But when I showed up in person, the price doubled. Remembering Peter's words in Coober Pedy, I have to insist on the agreed price or I'll turn around and go somewhere else. It works. As for the infection, it was cured by a Serbian doctor, but I am to rest it for a few days at least.

We spent some time in the secondhand bookshops of Russel, Bourke and Brunswick Streets, the soul of the city, with a nice atmosphere and a reputation as Australia's cultural centre and drug hub. Melbourne feels worldly. Coffee shops rather than clubs, trams rather than buses and the down-to-earth attitude of the people mean you won't feel like you're in just another megalopolis for a while. A little Italian, a little Greek, in fact every other nationality can be found here. There are also plenty of places to eat, drink a good coffee or just lie under a tree and read a book for hours.

This Seweryn guy was roughing it in the true sense. He must have had it tough, if only because of his almost unpronounceable first name, so dangerously close to 'sewer' or 'swearing' in English. It would have been very vulnerable to the snide remarks and smirks of the badass population of the vagrant camp sites of the goldfields. Never revealed in his book, we do not know by what name he was actually called, or whether he had a nickname. Against all odds, he could have proudly called himself a successful documentarist, had he ever known the term. He was incredibly modest and humble and never expected to be recognised as a writer. According to him, his texts—only excerpts of which have been translated into English—were for leisure, for killing time, not for serious reading.

This is exactly what I do under a canopy of trees in Melbourne's Kings Domain, not far from the banks of the Yarra River, when suddenly my eyelids grow heavy and I feel myself starting to doze off.

54
Eureka I have found it: How Much Does a Dream Cost

It's 1854 and I am at a campfire at Jim Crow fields, in what will once become Dalesford, Victoria. Two years ago I arrived to Australia on a boat spending three months on open seas.

Our cart that we had brought from London fell apart only a few kilometres on the local road, the mare we bought as a bargain refused to cooperate only few miles outside the town and didn't understand any commands in our language. We virtually ran out of money after only two weeks spent by the river in Melbourne under tents in preparation for the journey to the mines. We could not afford a hotel. While in Cape of Good Hope you paid 2 shillings for a room with lunch and dinner per day, in Melbourne they ask 2 pounds sterling for a room shared with two others, no food included.

In general, everything is six times dearer than in Europe and things are scarce, even fruits and vegetables, which were so plentiful in every port on the way to Australia, are nowhere to be seen or overpriced. In Australia, we paid for water for the first time in our lives. Two gallons cost 1 shilling, that's like 9 liters for $40 if I was here 170 years later. I know this because I can tie any price to gold: 1 ounce gold is worth about £4 pounds sterling which means that if you devide the price of 1 oz of gold at any time in the future by four, you get the exchange rate of the pound sterling in my time. For example, if an ounce of gold costs about AU$3,000 in 2024, my pound sterling would be worth around AU$750. In my time we don't have cents but we have shillings and pennies. A shilling is 1/20th of a pound sterling, a penny is 1/12th of a shilling. Besides, I was born in the Austrian Empire. I am used to guldens and ducats and I don't have a calulator. They don't exist. I have a good brain though, a fountain pen and paper.

I can get a horse for £60, a cow for £20, a cart of £40 and even buy 1 acre of bush for £1 but a minimum subdivision of land allowed for sale is 80 acres. If I had a lot of money I could buy unlimited land unlike in America where I would only be allowed to buy so much but a lot cheaper. This was deliberate and made many settlers bankrupt because no money was left for sheds, plough and supplies and the first harvest was far away and very uncertain.

One bushel of oats for the horse is about 2 pounds and will last three days. Like petrol for your car in the distant future you need to buy it constantly when on the road. £80 is a price for the first class on an ocean steamer if I ever want to go back to Europe in comfort or it's £35 economy. I can have my tooth pulled for £1 or buy a good dog for £5 and a better one for £10. A local black fellow tried to sell me his lubra once. He asked one shilling.

They ask one shilling for a quart of milk, one shilling for a loaf of bread. Because washing machines haven't been invented yet, laundry is a service. A price of laundering a shirt is the same as the cost of new shirt in England.

I am looking after my own possessions and am solely responsible for my own safety. I pay 30 shillings a month and then what I dig from the ground is mine but I need to protect it against people called bushrangers—criminals operating in the bush often ambushing caravans. So, a good dog is priceless. My Wisla's barking is a sign to them that I will be prepared to give them a warm welcome.

I also need to be aware of fraudsters trying to sell their stakes in mines that no longer have any gold in them. They are very inventive and cunning. If you're not careful, you can spend all your possessions on an empty shell. I lost £150 once in a financial speculation and that really hurt.

It takes me three days to see the smoking chimneys of Port Phillip Bay if I walk to Melbourne or pay half a pound to hire a cart. 75ml of cognac costs £1, but the sale of alcohol is strictly controlled and regulated and there is a thriving black market. Whereas in England I can earn 2 shillings per day, in Australia I expect 10 to 12 shillings per day. That's why people come—for the money hidden in the ground. You can make a lot of money in Australia, but you can also lose everything. You have to be in good health and good spirits. We have zero inflation. Money, once you have it, keeps its purchasing power.

A good cook can earn seven pounds a week, a hired labourer can expect £1.5 a day. I tried my luck as a storekeeper too but there is a £15 upfront quarterly tax and that spoils the game. I earned fifty something pounds in three months this way. A government official earns from £300 which can go up to £700 if you're a gold commissioner. This job however is only reserved for lads from good English families. They are the guys who collect my taxes. The yearly salary of Charles La Trobe the governor on the other hand is £15,000. He's just been replaced by Charles Hotham in a pompous celebration.

The Postman arrives every Sunday with news from Europe. We all look forward to it. The siege of Sevastopol is of particular interest to us because the Crimean War is nearing its climax as the British, French and their allies push for the strategic Russian port. They're using the Turks as a battering ram against the Russians. Control of the Black Sea is the goal. The Tsar's fleet is in the port and the British are determined to deny him access to the Mediterranean. It's funny. To this day, I haven't met a single Englishman who isn't convinced of the invincibility of the British army. I wish I could see their mugs in fifty years. There is friendly rivalry between England and America raging right now with the first feeling that the latter might start to surpass them soon in some areas such as the maritime transport.

I made myself a broth of a cockatoo today. The soups from parrots are okay but perhaps it is just hunger that adds flavour to them. You don't eat them very often. The birds are skinny but wear the most beautiful gown of feathers. One feels almost guilty when plucking them out of their skin. Possums are better but only blackfellas can catch them during the day. They know all the tricks. Their trackers can even find a dead person at the bottom of a pond by merely looking at its surface. It is quite unbelievable how sharp their senses are.

A visitor arrives to sit with me at the campfire. I know him. He was here before.

"Hey, Sew, have you been to the meeting this morning?" he asks.

"No. Did I miss anything?" I reply.

"You know there is a strong initiative now to raise against the rule. It's happening soon, it's inavitable."

"Yes, I know. Why would I do that?"

We both give each other a lengthy look. We've been throught that conversation before.

"Well, the conditions became hardly bearable now, the tax burden is at its highest, many of us can't make ends meet, we want the tax be paid from the gold exports rather than diggings, they shouldn't have the blank check to send it all to England but use it for building roads and stuff. Can't you see what's happening? La Trobe made a thousand of promises then quietly cashed in and disappeared in Switzerland. Now the bludger Hotham is sucking us dry. He was all hope but he ended up disaster. He reduces salaries, suspends staff, lowers rations. Yeah, he's extending his mansion by a reception hall and builds a brick wall around it. He stopped fixing roads, the land is more expensive than ever, in short, the guy is a thug. He may know how to run a boat but certainly not a country. We're going to become a nation like Americans, people are ready to fight. You are an ex-soldier, you have experience, I ask you again, come with us."

We sit in silence for a good few minutes watching the fire slowly burn.

"Well, I don't wear your ribbon, I don't attend your meetings but I also don't pay taxes. I don't want my brothers to burn my tent down. I work hard in my mine and mind my business. You do me great honour, for which with equal openness, I must reply to you that I will neither organise you nor guide you. At a time when almost all countries treated me as a bastard there was only one English government in Europe that gave me a refuge. Sorry fellows. I didn't come here to fight the British."

"You're not being fair," he says.

"Look. Besides, have you considered what you want to achieve? Have you weighed up the resources that the country has and whether they are sufficient to maintain independence? Now, even if you somehow did overthrow the government, how long would you last? Any squadron would come to Port Phillip, put ashore a few thousands troops with a battery of cannons. You, with such a weak force, having no real weapons, do you thik that all those magnificent speakers with music playing along would stand the fire? And have you asked others in towns if they want to share such freedom with you? They may not want to take part in it. You talk about freedom, yet, the meetings only mention taxes and deputies. No my friend, this country has a potential but its time hasn't come yet. You need to be self-sufficient first. Until then, you will never trully be independent."

The rebellion was brutally crushed. The Eureka Stockade was an expensive dream that ended up in disaster. It faded into oblivion leaving a wound that never really healed. Almost two centuries later, in the beautiful city of Melbourne, the legacy of Sir Charles Hotham will hang over the metropolis like a big cloud of fog on a rainy day. The Australian political system will be built on a tradition of no open criticism of authority and the era of powerful governors will gradually give way to an era of tinpot state premiers.

In 2020 one of them—a self-righteous nerd—will hijack personal responsibility for your own safety and abuse emergency powers in the name of public health. There will be a very thin line between freedom and oppression. He will lock people down in their homes for a year and use paramilitary squads to quash protests. He will threaten with draconian fines and jail time. Victoria is going to become the most culturaly rich but also the most nanny-like state in the Australian Commonwealth with the reputation for the worst public finances, authoritarian practices and little accountability for politicians.

It's almost five in the afternoon when I wake up with what feels like a bad hangover. The evening silhouette of Melbourne is breathtaking. There's a light breeze, the birds are chirping their southern cross songs and it's time for dinner. The pub where we go to has a large poster on the wall. Chopper is doing an evening show.

55
Uncle Chopper And Papa Rog

Although most Australians today like to think of themselves as normal, civilised people, many overseas visitors still associate them with images of their ancestors being dragged in chains on wooden ships somewhere in England. The ex-penal colony stigma is still alive and kicking, all in the context of: Yeah, yeah, they did wrong, were deservedly punished and sent to the furthest known tip of the world to work their way back into society (wink, wink), but at the same time we'll get rid of them for good (chuckle, chuckle). Weren't the English clever? Two birds killed with one stone, as it were.

Meeting this kind of a criminal archetype in person, however, may be easier said than done. Criminals in contemporary Australia look much like their overseas counterparts: indiscernible from the average citizenry, and often very high up in the socio-economic and political hierarchy. They don't usually brag about being criminals. Quite the opposite. That is why the pub in one of the suburbs is full and packed to the last place. Tonight there are a few people who not only don't hide it, but are openly proud of it.

Mark Brandon Chopper Read, who once terrorised the underbelly of Melbourne, will always be remembered as an underrated celebrity. Being an upgraded, heavyweight version of the now largely obsolete Ned Kelly, Chopper is a glorified villain and the main star of the evening.

True, he didn't eat seven compatriots like Alexander Pierce back in 1822, but it doesn't mean the times have gone any sissier.

He famously had his ears cut off and became the central character of a successful movie. After serving his time, he became a hyped book author, selling a substantial number of copies, and he even wrote a spooky children's book.

His forerunner, a skinny type who looks like a host of a sleazy bogan program, whose name I have forgotten, takes to picking on the audience right from the start.

"What's your name, sir? Justin? Do you know why girls love you, Justin? Because they love you 'just in'.

"And are there any fucking Pommies tonight? What are you sir?

Some mumbled voices come from the audience.

"—yeah? What is it? Slovak? I never heard that in my life! Hardcore sense of humour you have over there, eh? And you?"

"Czech."

"Check what?

"Republic?"

A moment of silence.

"Any—any other fucking Republics? Banana Republic anyone? Are you still dropping bombs on each other or you laid down your weapons now?"

After a twenty-minute monologue, he introduces a guest. We have never seen him before. He is a decent-looking uncle with a nice cordial smile. He is clean-shaven and his name is Roger something Rogerson.

"Have you ever seen anybody with legs as skinny as that?" giggles the no name host. He sits on a stool with his microphone in his hand as if he is about to start telling children's stories. A bit disappointing for a show like that, we're thinking. This guy looks like he's just leaving for Sunday church.

"Ladies and gentlemen, a warm welcome for Dodger!" Audience applauding.

His first story is about a criminal who went on prison leave and was expected to make a move on a sports club. Dodger's party was waiting for him, and arrested him so convincingly that his head disappeared from his shoulders and his mother had to identify him by a curved toe.

"Nice lady, she really was. I felt sorry for her. I tried to cheer her up: if your son had gone by the protocol, nothing would have happened to him. He had signed a form asking if he was planning to commit any crimes while on leave." The most notorious guy Dodger had finished off was Warren Lanfranchi—a drug dealer from Sydney. He shot him dead in the street, point blank, and was acquitted because it was in 'self-defence'. Lanfranchi's girlfriend, a prostitute, Sallie-Anne Huckstepp didn't buy the story and turned it into a media circus, almost becoming a star until her body was found in a Centennial Park pond in Sydney's Eastern Suburbs. They never found out who had done this and Dodger got a bravery award. He used to head a police hold-up squad in his famous days, and had been a highly regarded cop.

"I got a tip-off from our guy, leading me to a young fellow who had been getting around raping children around Petersham. I sorted him out with my gun, but unfortunately he was a son of a police official who ranked higher than I at the time, and he was giving me hard times ever after."

He offers a moral to the story. "Then one day I found he had finally died. I went to his funeral and when everybody was gone, I pissed all over his grave."

Dodger only went to jail after he had—kind of—botched the shooting of his rival police officer. His pals didn't do it right. He says he's always looked up to his work mates who made millions drug trafficking. He was never anywhere near it. He was famously released after serving a year or so, and he'd be successfully dodging until this day, had he not forgotten, some time later in 2014, that in this new age of technology, surveillance cameras were virtually everywhere, and they would record him if he's trying to get rid of a corpse in a storage unit. Completely underestimating the investigative skills of his younger colleagues by trade, he and his buddy, another ex-cop, didn't go to great lengths to clean their tracks after the murder of a young drug trafficker. With that, he finally embraced jail as his permanent home: in 2016, he is sentenced to life and he is going to die in prison in 2024. Of course, when we sit in the pub and listen to his stories, we don't know that yet.

Next, there is an auction. There are items for sale, all signed by Chopper, who we still haven't seen after two-thirds of the program. A four-kilo axe, signed by Chopper, a large butcher knife signed by Chopper, colour posters of Chopper sitting on a chopper signed by Chopper, an authentic photograph of the dead Turk who Chopper shot in the eye in the final scene of the movie, after being led for execution to the wrong car park. Also signed by Chopper.

"Come on, pussies! Don't make this hard!" the host says. "Just think of the huge resale potential of these memorabilia!"

The highlight of the evening has finally arrived. Chopper himself with a beer can in his hand.

"Well, first of all, the movie isn't true, it's eighty per cent true but twenty per cent fucking bullshit. I've never beaten up my girlfriend and her name was not Tanya. I was never a shill like I was portrayed in the movie. That wouldn't work. I wouldn't have gotten away with something like that eh. Anyway, I'm lucky I'm still alive." He drinks beer.

"Where was I. Oh, yeah, I was gonna tell you how they chopped off my ears. That was brutally true in the movie. The whole prison had turned against me and I wouldn't live long if I didn't do something, right? And I had to show them I was mad enough to justify transfer because they said I wasn't going anywhere! And what's better than chopping your own ears off to prove your point, right? One of my mates was doing it, while others were watching, and when he was halfway through the first ear, I felt this warm water trickling down my neck, except it wasn't water, it was blood, right? I said to him, 'What the fuck are you doing?' And he says, 'I'm trying to be gentle, mate". And I say to him, calmly, that if he's hacking my fucking ear off, he can't do it gently like that, because it fucking hurts! It hurts like hell! And so he did the other one real quick."

He drinks beer.

"Yeah, when they cut your ears, there's blood everywhere. Tarantino fucked that all up in his *Reservoir Dogs*. There wasn't a single drop of blood. He should have consulted me, I'm a fucking ear-chopping authority, ain't I? I had chopped my ears off well before anybody even bloody heard of Tarantino."

He drinks beer.

"And they didn't even invite me to the screening, though it was all about me. Bana called me and said if I wasn't going, he wasn't going, but all the others didn't want me there because they knew if I was there all the journos would stay clear of them, cos they'd all be around *me*, right? And I didn't make a fucking cent from the movie. They ripped me off! They would get their hands on it anyway, so I just transferred the dough to fucking children's hospitals, but then I had second thoughts and politely asked them to pay it back, but I tell you, you don't fuck with children's hospitals. Don't even try it. But no hard feelings. I do like children. Really do."

He drinks beer.

"Do you want to ask me anything?"

"How do you like your imitators, like Ronnie Johns. He does it right, doesn't he—?" somebody asks from the crowd.

"This guy's a wanker. I don't talk like Ronnie Johns, do I? That's not my voice, the speed, is it?" He makes some gestures.

"I bumped into him once and I told him, 'If you want to be like me, chop your ears off, mate, have the guts, otherwise you'll always be a fake.'"

He drinks beer.

"Another question?"

"Would you say anything to the filmmakers if you met them in the street?" somebody from the crowd asks.

"Yeah, where is me fucking money, ya bastards!"

Chopper died in 2013.

VIII. Melbourne to Sydney

56
Mister Ricketts' Beautiful Soul

If we wanted, we could be in Sydney in one day now. But we prefer the roads less travelled that will stretch it for three more weeks. Pure chance gets us to the Dandenong Ranges, east of Melbourne, where a true sanctuary can be found. William Ricketts dedicated his entire life to clay sculptures. This is a place of tranquillity, mystique and meditation[57]. He wanted it that way—low-key—he did not live for publicity. A winding road takes us to stalls selling local produce, such as honey or flowers, all unattended: just put your money in the box and take your stuff. The price list is next to it. As we enter a small enclosure, hidden by the greenery of the surrounding forest, we enter another planet, one that has little in common with the outside world.

Kingdom of peace

The entrance is guarded by two well-built Aboriginal leaders on big boulders, and all around the garden there are faces, busts, hands, and body shapes. Here is a character peeking out of a tree, there is another stepping out of a stone, they crawl in and out of their rocky ambience, all in perfect harmony with their surroundings. There are warriors, mothers, children, and all their faces have the smallest details, showing strong emotions, some of them quite chilling.

Ricketts transcended into the Aboriginal soul. At least that's how he felt towards the end of his life. He talks about his visions from a small television screen. He bought this land in the 1920s and called it Potter's Sanctuary. He worked on it all his life and this is his legacy: a lush, green, friendly kingdom of radiant energy, mystery and stillness.

We borrow a bit of that energy and head over the hills to the High Country, along the same winding road that brought us here.

57
North Over the Hill Country

If you're heading north from Victoria to New South Wales, it's either the motorway or the country. We opt for the country and head for Wangaratta. There is something special about walking around this beautiful landscape knowing so few people are in the area. Our next friends live in a small house on a green hillside. They have dogs that run around the house chasing anything that moves. This time it was an echidna. They have sniffed it out and it is now buried in the ground with only the top few spines sticking out.

Mount Buffalo is not far from here—a Victorian Alpine National Park. Snow chains are mandatory for all conventional cars in September and we're risking a fine. Back in the city it didn't occur to me we might ever need them. They're expensive, the weather is perfectly dry and we're just passing through. Given the situation, we decide it's overkill.

Colac Colac near Corryong is the last stop in Victoria, then the mountain pass takes us to Australia's First State: New South Wales.

Typical mountain road, Victoria/NSW border

The border to New South Wales is on the Alpine Way Road in the Snowy Mountains and it goes up and down steeply. This is quite a lot of work for our car brakes. They start to burn and smell badly, screaming, "Give us a break, man!" And we do. Quite frequently.

Snow covers gum trees by the roadside but the road is nice and dry. The Alpine National Park gradually gives way to the Snowy Mountains and then Kosciuszko National Park near a town called Khancoban. The highest official peak lies somewhere in the vicinity.

Whether it is Australia's highest point as such is debatable, as there are three significantly higher peaks in Australia's Overseas Territories, Mount McClintock and Mount Menzies in Antarctica, and Mawson Peak on the small islands of Heard and McDonald.

But they are far, far away and so Mount Kosciuszko can enjoy a sweet monopoly. Some people might laugh at its height, but come here in winter and walk it up in snow. These are our thoughts in Jindabyne, where having replenished supplies, we're set for the mountains.

58
Why Mount Kosciuszko

The original plan was to hire skis—standard cross-country skis—and avoid the chairlift at all costs, because explorers don't use them. Then get to a place called Dead Horse Gap walk up the ten kilometres or so, and then return. The first problem is that the information ladies don't want to tell you much beyond the official touristy claptrap. "Are you very, very, very experienced?" one of them asks with a worried look, as if we had asked for something illegal.

We buy a topographic map. The ski rental announces that normal cross-country skis are out of the goddamn question, they're not renting them to us under any circumstances. We need sturdier back-country skis. They don't want to have anything to do with our broken limbs.

"It's this or nothing," a Swiss guy in the ski rental says. "You need to buy a compass. We're not renting it."

"We're only going straight up and then straight down," I try to be joke but I sound somewhat stupid.

"Yeah, yeah, look, I'll at least show you where to go," he replies.

Ngariro Campground is within the national park border. We drive there for the night so that we can start very early the next day. Ice patches cover the tent canvas in the morning.

There are tall snow poles, but other than that it's a map and common sense. Most people just want to take the chairlift to the top, walk the rest and tick off the continent's highest mountain. Thredbo is their refuge. It's excellent for seasonal dads with kids chained to their legs, but a bit boring for someone who wants to get a better idea of the area, especially if you want to create conditions closer to those of the early explorers. Those who want lower prices go to Jindabyne. Forewarned is forearmed. We can do without Thredbo.

On the way up the highest mountain

The morning is very foggy and there's hardly any light. We put on our boots and skis and put some warm clothes in our rucksacks as the temperature is minus one degree Celsius. We take plenty of water, food and the industrial gloves we used to castrate corn in Kununurra. They are greenish and worn but will do the job. We've forgotten two of the most important things in the car, but we don't know it yet.

The climb is steep at first, so it's more of a march than a ski. We need to get higher onto the mountain ridge and then pull through a thick eucalyptus forest. After about an hour, the trail becomes slightly less demanding, with trees thinning out and shrubs and smaller gum trees appearing. Here and there larger rocks and boulders emerge, and we follow the ski path made by more adventurous people before us.

Final ascent to Mount Kosciuszko, NSW

In a few hours the fog is almost gone, visibility improves but the sky is still nowhere in sight. Metabolism has kicked in and the cold feeling from the morning disappeared. After about two hours, we can see the first skiers from the Thredbo village. A wide open snowy plain is ahead, with occasional information signs partly or entirely covered in snow. The sun peeks briefly from behind the cloud curtain, but quickly pops back and stays put. Another hour and we're at the foot of the mountain; at least that's what we think, from a broken cluster of planks pretending to be a signpost. Mount Kosciuszko is not immediately recognisable. It even seems to be lower than the surrounding peaks, especially the one next to it—Mount Townsend, named after Thomas Townsend, the guy who later became First Viscount Sydney (after whom the largest city was named). Everything is under snow and so we take to the shortest path uphill, which points left. It's a slow ascent that takes at least an hour, and all of a sudden the sun crawls from under the cloud and decides to stay. After locating a ski track again, the ascent becomes easier. We're almost at the top.

In 1839 Sir Paul Edmund Strzelecki[58] came here with two English companions, James Riley and James McArthur, and two Aboriginal guides "Charlie" and "Jackie". They were here to map the highest point of the land.

"There we are gents, the highest peak of New Holland!"

"New South Wales," somebody corrects.

"No, of the lot I think—Australia," Sir Edmund insists.

"Shall we say something for the record?" says one of them to lift the mood.

They look at one another not knowing what to say.

"Won't go any higher, will it, Jackie? You reckon?"

"No," says the Aboriginal guide.

Silence.

"Soooo, it's this one over there, is it?" Riley starts again.

"Naaa, the one on the left," replies McArthur.

"Charlie?"

"Yeah, it's that one."

They are quiet again gasping for air.

"Well, not much to look at is it?" McArthur says finally, with a frown.

"What are we puttin' it down as?" says Riley again. They all turn their eyes into the map and then back on the mountain.

"It looks like a bloody tomb I saw back home in Krakow," says Strzelecki to the general bemusement of the others.

"What was the name of it? Riley asks after he finished chuckling.

"Yeah, sure! 'Kosciuszko'. Gipps will be over the moon about this. He can't even pronounce *my* name let alone this."

He packs his stuff back in his rucksack and is quiet for a moment.

"Do you know what's long and hard that a bride gets when she marries a Polish guy?" Sir Edmund continues.

Nobody has a clue.

"Her new last name," says Sir Edmund as he gives command to his fellows to start packing and return.

Mount Kosciuszko[59], 2,228 m ASL

The sun is at its best now as we foolishly enjoy it, forgetting completely about sunburn. We're going to bitterly regret it only a few hours later. We didn't bother taking sun cream and sun glasses because the weather was so hopelessly bad in the morning. A silly mistake.

There is a handful of people at the top, their skis stuck deep in snow and all having a warm cuppa. There's nothing better than hot tea after a long walk to a freezing mountain peak. The descent is steep at first, then it evens out, but the path that brought us here has disappeared. It all looks different now. Knowing that down there somewhere must be a river, we can't go too wrong. Entering the thick forest with legs waist-deep in snow, our green gloves frozen gloves and our faces are brutally, brutally burned.

It starts with a warm heat all around the head in the evening. By night there are water blisters around the cheeks, and by morning the skin is stinging and hurts badly, all over our faces. Our eyes are constantly teary, red and sore. We can't sleep and our vision is blurred. Snow blindness. We somehow get to Jindabyne and spend the whole next day there to pull ourselves together.

Driving on the following day is very difficult. We stop to pick up a suicidal turtle lying in the middle of the road. The landscape is changing now. What was lush and green becomes monotonously brown and yellow. The mountains on the other side of the Great Dividing Range don't get as much water. And so yellow is a word that has just been promoted.

Yellow: that's the presage of Canberra.

59
Canberra in a Nutshell

To make up for the yellow monotony that Canberra is surrounded with from each direction, the capital organises an annual flower festival called Floriade. Flowers are everywhere, of all kinds and all shapes. The more colours the better.

Canberra is a town made with one thing in mind: to represent. Beautiful for some, ugly for others, it's spread out like a middle-aged chubby wife on a public beach, knowing that guys will notice but not touch. A bit like a marvel of technology, designed on a board, man-made, although in all its fairness, pretty avant-garde and bold. The large roundabouts visible from the Parliament Hill pour out into long and wide parallel streets. The 'layout' town is probably best enjoyed from the Telstra tower. The city was designed for a million people or so but only about one third of that number live there, enough prominents for the prices to keep up with Sydney and Melbourne—mainly government small and bigwigs. One of our friends told us once that if we ever stumble upon Canberra and can't find anywhere to sleep, we can try to take a few pictures of the American or Israeli embassies. They would find me accommodation. But we're not into cities. They don't exist yet. We're discovering Australia.

60
Mountains Upside Down

If you were an inmate in your average Australian prison, you would want 'Goulburn' on your CV. The city of Goulburn has a reputation for having one of the toughest supermaximum security prisons in the country, housing all sorts of the most fearsome criminal elements and most notorious names. It was a home of Ivan Milat until his death in 2019. It sits on a hill and would have a generous view of the city if the guys had windows.

There is also the Big Merino. It stands by the road as a symbol of a once profitable industry. The wool business has been sabotaged by fake cheap synthetics and has gone out of fashion. If I want a good wool jumper and a coffee, this is probably where I will go. There is also a small museum that tells me a lot about wool—the material.

Big Merino, Goulburn, NSW

About seventy-five per cent of them are merinos, the rest are crossbreeds. The Merino was imported from Spain and has been here for as long as anyone can remember—that is, the end of the eighteenth century. The breed has toughened up in incredibly harsh conditions to become probably the most resilient domestic animal of all time. The next step up in toughness would be the surface of the moon.

As we drive out of town, I can't help but notice the dry fields with no grass, big brown dusty patches of scorched earth from weeks of endless sun and not a drop of rain. The address we look for reads: "Turn left to Kialla, follow the dirt road until you find an old large fridge. That's our mailbox. Then follow the road uphill until you reach our house."

Keith is a double of George W. Bush—in appearance at least. He lives in an old farm-house and has lots of cows that chew on anything they can find during the hot day: the yellow sun-burnt grass that dominates the local countryside and silage he throws them from his tractor every evening.

"I had a mowing business in Sydney a while ago, but I bailed out. The city is not for me any more," he says. He lives with his girlfriend who still works in Sydney—that is only about two and a half hours away from here. He lights up a cigarette and looks like everybody can just kiss his arse. Nothing will throw him off balance. He owns the whole forest nearby. It's going to be his retirement when the time comes.

"Where are you going next," he asks. That is actually a good question.

"Go to the mountains."

Mountains inverted: Wollemi, NSW

Kanangra Boyd is the closest national park on the way north. On the map it is an incredibly vast green patch south west of Sydney. It's got a karst area called Jenolan Caves which is worth a stop. There is another and even a bigger green patch about two hours north called Wollemi National Park. Most Australians on hearing that name will say something like: "Oh yeah, that's where they found the prehistoric tree."

The Wollemi Pine was discovered by chance in 1994, when a hiker venturing into the remotest parts of the park found himself in an isolated deep gorge, set apart from the rest of the bush by terrain. "This is a nice tree," he thought. Nothing like anything he had seen before. He brought back a sample. *Wollemia nobilis* has survived since Jurassic time, which was about two hundred million years ago. They say there are only about hundred of them in the wild and only a small circle of insiders know where the place is: a public secret. One day this planet might be without people again, but the nobilis could still be alive. To understand it better, you can put it on a timeline. If the Wollemi Pine existed for only 24 hours, the entire known history of mankind would start about twenty seconds ago.

Oil shell refinery ruins in Newnes

The entire area of the Wollemi National Park are inverted mountains. In Europe, people settled in the valleys first and then went up as far as the conditions allowed. Here, it's the other way round and so when you hike, you leave civilisation when you descend into canyons. The mountains are vast and rugged. In 1981 a Cessna with five people on board crashed in Barrington Tops a mountain range north of Wollemi National Park. It was never found.

Sometimes you can drive down in places like Newnes, for example, which is also a road to the past. Somewhere hidden deep in the bush there are the ruins of an oil-shell factory. It was still in full swing at the beginning of the twentieth century. Oil-shell rock was first destructed here then distilled and pumped up the hill for further processing. Its ruins are now covered by moss and grass and are gradually being claimed back by nature to become one again.

There is also a large campsite surrounded by high rock walls near a decomissioned railway tunnel that is now home to glow worms. When you go inside, it's like a perfectly black night sky with thousands of stars and planets.

Glow Worm Tunnel[60]

Tomorrow we're going west again for one last time. Because there is a place in New South Wales where time simply stopped: Hill End.

IX. Big Smoke

61
Where Freedom Begins: Hill End

Just as Western Australia had its pearling industry, South Australia its opal glory, Victoria and New South Wales had their gold rushes. While the gold settlements in Victoria later merged into larger townships, in New South Wales they were simply abandoned. Towns sprang up in a matter of decades and then all but disappeared. We head to Hill End, which in 1873 was the second largest town in New South Wales with a population of about thirty thousand. The history is the town and the town is the history.

Today it's just a dot on the map with nothing but hills around it, and it feels like the end of the world. There are only three roads to get there: The first from Mudgee, the second from Bathurst through another gold-mining hub called Sofala, and the third and roughest from Bathurst through the hills called the Bridle Track. It used to be a horse trail.

Our hatchback does quite well on the 4WD-only track, but the truth is, it's not so comfortable. The road goes uphill along quite a steep rock face, and occasionally it narrows due to falling rocks. A huge boulder would fall on it, about halfway to the town, at a place called Monaghan's Bluff. It would be closed for years and reopened only in 2023.

The Bridle Track goes up and down until it reaches a causeway through Turon River. We're rather tired by then. The weather is hot again as we move north and the river offers plenty of shade. We're just about to jump in it when an old 4x4 arrives. From Bathurst we passed no more than two or three cars, but none of them driven by a hippie woman with four dogs sitting by her side. She pulls down her window.

"Do we know you?" she asks in a bored voice. Their large German shepherds stopped breathing and wait for further instructions.

"Oh, hi there. How are you. I don't think so," I say, somewhat unsure what to say.

The dogs now start to bark loudly.

"Well. Who cares! Let's have a swim," she replies with a smile and slowly drives through the causeway to the other side. Before we know it, she has stripped off her clothes and she and the dogs are splashing around in the water. The huge tattoo just above her mons is clearly visible from the other side of the river.

Remote hills between Bathurst and Hill End, NSW

After driving up the last bit from the river to the town, we find ourselves in the second half of the nineteenth century. New South Wales was about to end its penal transports and, as conditions for ordinary people began to improve, it opened up to immigration, and not just from Britain. The immigrants were typically poor and the new country didn't enjoy a good reputation. It didn't have an official name and was regarded as a second-class country, where people went out of desperation rather than choice. And their motivation grew with the knowledge that this new world offered rare new opportunities.

Catalogued by Dmitri Mendeleev in his periodic table in 1869 as Au, gold has been known by humanity for thousands of years. It's about the only material that can withstand whims of time and its supply cannot be artificially inflated as the only way to produce it is to dig it from the ground. It is universal store of value and the most reliable form of money. The periods of gold rush in the middle of the 19th century were not easy times and for many this was the only way to gain economic independence. In quite the literary sense, they came to dig it from the ground. Gold was the ticket to freedom.

The smallest continent might be young in political terms, but when it comes to geology it's the oldest grandma in town. A few hundred million years ago, the earth's plates moved and caused huge eruptions, which then hurled a large numbers of liquid rocks called quartz to its surface. With quartz, they also released smaller amounts of metal 'dirt'. After the eruptions cooled down, the rock then hardened and the small particles got into rivers, more precisely into their lowest layers, because gold is heavier than anything around it.

The first mentions of gold in Australia are said to have come from Portuguese maps. They marked the north-west coast as Costa d'Ouro. Nobody knows why, but this continent has always been associated with gold. If Cook had dug a few hundred metres under his flag in Queensland, he would have found a field containing two and a half thousand ounces of gold.

For a long time, however, the publication of such information was considered taboo. As early as 1823, a certain James McBrien stumbled upon gold while exploring rivers, then Edmund Strzelecki did the same during his geological studies, as did William Branwhite Clarke around 1841. The governor at the time, Sir George Gipps, kindly advised them all to keep their mouths shut because he knew only too well what a ragtag bunch of hoodlums that news would attract.

The information was spread gradually and only after it had

been established that there was enough gold to support many people for many years.

The New South Wales mountains were impenetrable for a long time, and settlement started much later than on the coast. Bathurst was the first significant town outside Sydney that was founded inland, and had a certain peculiarity. The river flew west and not east to the sea, as would normally be expected. The first settlers thought that it might end in an unknown lake, and around 1815 they started to search for it. This was one of the reasons the Bridle Track was formed between Bathurst and another town called Wellington, to the west. It was later used for moving cattle herds, but Bridle Track was there long before gold was found here.

Then three gentlemen, Edward Hammond Hargraves, John Lister and James Tom, discovered in 1851 the first significant gold deposit in a place called Yorkies Creek, twenty-nine kilometres north east of Orange. Only then did the authorities realise that it could actually benefit the local land, and immigration was justified. Hargraves was rewarded and appointed Commissioner of Crown Lands, and while indulging in large quantities of rum—then the most valuable article in the colony—he had Yorkies Creek renamed for the biblical Ophir. He forgot his mates and let the new discovery be associated with his name only.

A short time later, gold was discovered in Dirt Holes Creek, near Tambaroora on the Turon River[61] on about a twenty-five kilometre stretch with Hill End in its middle. The twenty years that followed brought a gold rush of unimaginable proportions and an incredible boost to the local economy. Claiming just a small slice of the new riches was a shortcut to higher society.

62
It's Panning Out

We're going on a gold-panning tour with a guide who is going to show us what the business is about. We're to wait near the 'red chimney', the ruins of one of the local houses in a de facto ghost town called Tambaroora—outskirts of Hill End. Houses used to have chimneys and the solitary chimneys were usually what were left of the buildings long after people left and their houses fell apart. There are hardly any houses standing now. There is a spooky graveyard and deep cavities dug out all around the town are silent witnesess to its past.

Ted—who looks like the front page of a Lonely Planet guide—arrives in an old red Falcon, in dirty old leather hat. His wrinkly face is cleanly unshaven, he has a slow oscillating pace and is about seventy-five and pretty fit. In five minutes we're driving on a narrow dirt road to check the creek where he knows good spots. He gets out of his car, grabs his shovel and immediately begins to work. He digs deep in the river, scoops some debris into his black gold pan, separates the larger pieces with his gloves, throws stones and dirt away, then, with a fast flick of his hand takes the upper layer away and sloshes the rest in water. He then repeats the cycle a few more times until only a small amount of dirt stays in the pan. He keeps sloshing the remaining mud until only a spoonful of water resides on its bottom and somehow he separates only a few small dust particles, so that they stay on one side of the pan, not even a centimetre apart, while the rest of the worthless dirt gets chucked back into the creek. After that he licks his index finger, touches the dust gently, takes out a small water-filled ampoule, presses the finger on it, and shakes it gently. Finally, he seals it off with a plug.

"There you go. Gold." He says.

He does a few more rounds, then sits down. He lights up a cigarette, and comfortably leaning against a stump he continues.

"Gold is still in the river here but very little. After a hundred and fifty years, you know, not much is left. The trick is to get to the very bottom of the creek, through to the thickest mud layer where gold can't drop any further. It won't get under the clay. Then you just take it."

It looks easy. I try to imitate him but I fail miserably. My panning is slow and clumsy. Water in the pan is desperately dancing all over it, it splashes from side to side, as if saying to me in frustration, "What the hell is it that you want me to do?" In the first few pans I can't see anything at all.

Meanwhile, Ted sits nearby, smoking and watching. It takes me at least an eternity to finish one pan. My back hurts more and more after each one.

"Twenty-eight seconds a pan," he squeezes suddenly through his ciggy.

"Yeah, not me. I couldn't live on it," I admit. "How do you do it?"

"Years and years, mate."

I give up. There is no difference between mastering gold panning and playing the piano. Both require years of practising. Ted is a virtuoso.

There were a few categories of gold-diggers. Thousands of losers who sacrificed their health and life, and never really got anywhere. There were also those who found it, got rich, but no matter what they did after, we don't know anything about them because they left no trace. And finally, there were those who made it, prospered and documented it all for us. One of them was Bernard Otto Holtermann.

63
In Which Otto Won his Lotto

Otto Bernard Holtermann, a German immigrant from Hamburg, was a success story, a textbook example of what a person can achieve in the new world with a bit of luck and a lot of hard work.

He arrived around 1855 at the age of twenty. He did what he could with his limited English: jackaroo, photographic shop assistant and waiter in a Sydney hotel named after his home town. It was a well-known gold-digging community hub and it seemed the right place to be. That's where he met Hugo Luis Beyers from Posen, who already knew a thing or two about Tambaroora. It was right next to Hill End, where the German Town district was.

Beyers and Holtermann got a prospecting claim on a land lot in Hill End. Their joint venture was called Star of Hope. They did it in their spare time because they had to sustain themselves with other work. They looked after a hotel.

Hill End, NSW: 1873 versus present time

Life in Hill End wasn't easy. There were many who arrived only to scuttle back to Sydney before they could buy a pickaxe. The conditions were so harsh that Holtermann himself nearly lost his life when an explosion got out of control, almost burying him alive. It was a time of the second gold rush, when most gold lumps had already been extracted and what they now had to work with was alluvial gold in nuggets, found together with quartz. It was hard, debilitating work in which heavy specimens had to be pulled out of the ground for further processing. To finance operations, Beyers and Holtermann sold smaller shares to six other people, thus creating a syndicate. They did okay, but no breakthrough came until 12 October 1872, towards the very end of the gold rush. They pulled out a specimen of gold and quartz, the largest of its kind ever found. The lot weighed about three hundred kilograms, the gold yield was said to be about eighty-five kilos. After that they quit mining and started to do business. Beyers was later conned by a friend who had looked after his estate while he was away and eventually went broke, later returning to mining.

Holtermann was more successful: he imported goods from Germany, made and sold medicinal drops, entered politics and pursued his passion—photography, in those days a brand new and expensive discipline. He commissioned an extensive photo project with photographers Beaufoy and Merlin, capturing the life of ordinary people in the colonies. They successfully exhibited in Europe and America. After realising the power of pictures, he used a photo composition of himself with the golden nugget to market his products.

Interestingly enough, in those times of real economy, when *owning* was not confused with *owing*, he did not call himself a millionaire. It is estimated he owned about fifty kilograms of gold. Yet he built a few-storey, multi-room stone mansion with an elevated tower, overlooking Sydney Harbour, now unfortunately not accessible to public because it's owned by a posh Anglican private school called Shore.

Had he counted his blessings in today's inflated economy, his share of gold would have roughly got him a an ordinary, five-bedroom house in an average Sydney suburb. Times have changed and so has the purchasing power of money. Almost exactly two hundred years later, Mrs Governments will go on a wild binge with

Mr Banks and together they will send their former boss, Mr Gold, packing. This will happen when Nixon decouples gold from the dollar in 1971. They will teach everybody to count in six figures without the need of having any tangible wealth. Dirty sweated-in overalls will be replaced with shiny Versace suits.

But going back to Holtermann, he did buy a suit and became a member of parliament for St Leonards in 1883. During one of the meetings he apparently came up with a revolutionary idea:

"Tzz bridge von Milson's Point to Zydney? How'z that Gentlemen?"

He was laughed off. The nobility of the day just couldn't see the point. The Sydney Harbour Bridge saw the light of day in 1932, only fifty years later. Some say exactly at the coordinates he had envisioned.

Just when he had everything he ever wanted, and at the peak of his fame, he died of cancer at the age of only forty-seven. Holtermann's gold-digging success, however, was just a prelude to something much bigger. One hundred years later, in the 1950s, somebody searched an old shed and miraculously stumbled across three thousand perfectly preserved, extremely fragile glass plate negatives documenting, in the most vivid detail, the lives of the settlers in those times. If not for him and his gold the pictures would have never come into existence. They are priceless now and all exhibited at the Holtermann museum in Gulgong[62].

64
Epilogue

After two hours of teaching us how to get the remaining gold out of the creek, Ted only asks a few miserable dollars. We can't believe he's doing this almost for free. "Now bloody Centrelink makes sure you don't get rich. If you earn too much, they'll cut payments. My friend Rick earned a few bucks on the side and reported it. He's not doing it anymore. You have to like what you're doing. Every year I swear I'm done with it. But I still do it."

"I know people came here on school excursions," I say to him.

"Yeah, they've been coming for years. Kids from Sydney who only know concrete. Not like country kids. A Filipino girl asked me recently if I could lick her finger to scoop the gold dust from the pan, because the water was too dirty for her. Or there was a brat who threw my tools in the river. I had to search for them in the mud, waist-deep in water. And then he dobbed me in to his teacher when I sent him to the bus. Huge difference between city kids and country kids."

"So you're retired now?"

"Yeah but I am still doing things. I've been digging graves too. Now there's only two funerals a year. Terrible. It used to be much better."

The tip of the Holtermann's nugget is in the local private museum. The owner of History Hill,[63] with his beard down his belly button, shows us around his amazing lifetime creation. Ten thousand artefacts.

"I offered students free food and accommodation in exchange for archiving it. Not interested."

There is everything here; a replica of a long ventilation shaft, a geology expo, many tools of the period, spare parts, all kinds of containers, detailed description of trades of the time, old pictures, boxes, clothes, shoes, books, notes, even complete large machines that used to crush earth at day and night. Hill End used to be a noisy town. When the machines broke down, people couldn't sleep because the silence was so deafening.

We're sitting in the pub in the evening, the only one that has survived out of thirty others gone with the wind. A family of wallabies are grazing in sun that's going to set in a few minutes. They chew grass slowly. Squeaking sounds of birds can be heard from the trees behind them.

Where has everyone gone? Time really does seem to slow down after three months without distractions, flat screens, boring commercials, internet, email, socials, dates, meetings, daily routine. It's spiritually renewing. It has a calming effect on body and mind. If only for that one thing, it is definitely worth the effort. The most important discovery.

Everything is merging as if it had started yesterday, but I've lost exact count of the days. Maybe I should write it all down.

And maybe I should just forget it.

A few kilometres from here we're on the threshold of Sydney again, the semi-jovial, semi-pompous urban sprawl, where, because of the climate, you never know for sure if you're still on holidays weeks after coming back home, but where stress can catch up with you just like in any other place on earth. It forms from western, yellowish plains, gradually building up to form an agglomeration of subdivided land blobs that quickly make room for the ever-growing concrete suburbia, where houses stand in an orderly fashion, one next to another, and their small yards are neatly separated by high metal fences. Many fences.

And right behind all that is the shiny city—with high-rise appartments growing like mushrooms—that shows off its glamorous venues and tempts tourists with its icons, passing itself off as the real, true, and only dinky di image of the country.

FAR OUT. That's also Australia. But it's another story.

GLOSSARY

ABN – Australian Business Number

ANZAC – Australian and New Zealand Army Corps

ASL – above sea level

APC – Arms, Pits and Crotch; quick wash

Abo – a pejorative short for Aboriginal

billabong – a stagnant pool of water; dead-end of a stream or river

big smoke – any large city in Australia (originally Aboriginal description)

bindy, pl. bindies – sharp thorn, thorns in grass

bitumen - asphalt

bloke – slang for a male

bludger – a good-for-nothing; a lazy person

boab tree – an Australian tree unique to the Kimberley region; it has a thick trunk often in a shape of a bottle; 'bottle' tree

bogan – not very sophisticated, unrefined person; a chav (UK)

brownish – brown or similar (similarly gold*ish* – gold and similar, etc.)

CBD – City Business District

Centrelink – Australian welfare offices

chock-a-block – fully occupied; busy

croc – a crocodile

damper – simple Australian bread popular with swagmen

didgeridoo – a wind instrument of indigenous Australians

dinky-di - really, for real, speaking the truth, Australian slang

dirt road – gravel road

dodgy – something of questionable quality

dough – money; cash

dugout – a house or other underground property

dunny, pl. dunnies – slang for a toilet, bog

duty of care – a moral or legal obligation to ensure the safety or well-being of others

fair enough – used to admit that something is reasonable or acceptable; okay, I agree

far out – cool

Freo – a nickname for Fremantle (a town in Western Australia)

freshie – a freshwater crocodile

fruitcake – an eccentric mad person; a nutter

goodie – a good or favoured character

goon – cheap Australian wine bought in a cardboard box

hatch – a short for hatchback car

humpy – a small, temporary shelter made from bark and tree branches, traditionally used by Australian Aboriginals

inselberg – an island mountain

jackaroo – a young man working on a sheep or cattle station

legend – a person revered for something; often *fucking legend* to describe somebody who is absolutely cool or excessively proud or complacent

lilo – to ride an inflatable mattress on a running stream of water

lubra - Aboriginal woman

morning tea – a small meal or snack eaten between breakfast and lunch

mozzies – mosquitoes

nanny state – an overprotective system that tries to prevent everything before it happens

noodling – rummaging in piles of dirt and rubble to find opal

NSW – New South Wales

NT – Northern Territory

odo – odometer

Pollywaffle – Australian chocolate bar brand; a popular name to describe a piece of shit because it's brown and it's about the same size

potch – opal without much colour or worth

Powerball – a successful Australian lottery game modelled on its American namesake

PR – permanent residency

Qantas – Australian flag carrier company; the largest Australian airline

QLD – Queensland

redback – a small venomous spider

relly, pl. rellies – relative, relatives

roo – a short for kangaroo

saltie – a saltwater crocodile

SA – South Australia

Skip – an Anglo-Saxon Australian, a synonym for a "fair dinkum" Aussie, derived from the Australian TV show 'Skippy' starring a Kangaroo from the Australian bushland

spinifex – sharp-pointed Australian grass

spud – a potato

strewth – an exclamation used to express surprise or dismay, short for "God's truth"

sheila – slang for a female

Telstra – a big telecom company often known for its recalcitrant attitude

thongs – light sandals with a thong between the big end second toe, slippers, jandals (NZ), flip-flops (UK)

tradie, pl. tradies – a tradesman, tradesmen

tucker – Australian slang for food

VIC – Victoria

WA – Western Australia

whinger – a constantly complaining person

Map

Noteworthy Mountaints and Peaks

Mount McClintock; 3,490 m ASL, the Australian Antarctic Territory

Mount Menzies; 3,355 m ASL, the Australian Antarctic Territory

Mawson Peak; 2,745 m ASL, the Heard and McDonald Islands

Mount Kosciuszko; 2,228 m ASL, Snowy Mountains, NSW

Mount Townsend; 2,209 m ASL, Snowy Mountains, NSW

Mount Sonder / Rwetyepme; 1.380 m ASL, West MacDonnell Ranges, NT

Mount Meharry / Wirlbiwirlbi; 1245 m ASL, Karijini National Park, WA

Mount Bruce / Punurrunha; 1,234 m ASL, Karijini National Park, WA

St Mary Peak / Ngarri Mudlanha; 1,171 m ASL, Ikara-Flinders Ranges, SA

Mount Nameless / Jarndunmunha; 1,128 m ASL, Karijini National Park, WA

Mount Conner / Atilla; 859 m ASL, near Uluru, NT

Mount Stapylton, Grampians / Gariwerd; 244 m ASL, VIC

Hollow Mountain, Grampians / Gariwerd; around 240 ASL, VIC

Mount Arapiles / Djurite; around 140 m ASL, VIC

Mount Warning / Wollumbin, 1159 m ASL, NSW

Route and Refuelling

Day | From | To (km) | Total (km) | Full tank (X) | Spare fuel jerry can (x)

1 | Perth - Balcatta | 33 | 33 | X

2 | Perth Balcatta - Pinnacles | 287 | 320

Pinnacles - Jurien Bay | 49 | 369 | X

3 | Jurien Bay - Geraldton | 207 | 576 | X

Geraldton - Neren Neren | 184 | 760

4 | Neren Neren - Overlander Roadhouse | 94 | 854

Overlander Roadhouse - Carnarvon | 210 | 1064 | Xx

5 | Carnarvon - Exmouth/Lighthouse Carpark | 281 | 1354

6 | Exmouth - Cape Range National Park | 152 | 1497 | X

7 | Exmouth   Nanutarra Roadhouse | 210 | 1707

Nanutarra Roadhouse - Paraburdoo | 369 | 2076 | X

Paraburdoo - Tom Price | 80 | 2156

8 | Tom Price - Karijini NP/Savannah | 109 | 2265 | X

9 | Karijini NP/Savannah - Karijini/Dales | 55 | 2320

10 | Karijini NP/Dales - Mt. Bruce | 194 | 2514

11 | Karijini NP/Dales - Auski Roadhouse | 83 | 2597

Auski Roadhouse - South Hedland | 262 | 2859 | X

12 | Port Hedland - Sandfire Roadhouse | 216 | 3075 | Xx

13 | Sandfire Roadhouse - Broome/Roebuck | 290 | 3365

Broome/Roebuck - Broome | 58 | 3423 | Xx

14 | Broome - Willare Bridge Roadhouse | 166 | 3589

Willare Bridge Roadhouse - Fitzroy Crossing | 245 | 3834 | X

15 | Fitzroy C'/Geiki Gorge NP - Halls Creek | 350 | 4184 | X

Halls Creek (China Wall) - Spring Creek | 70 | 4254 | X

16 | Spring Creek Rest Area - Turkey Creek | 187 | 4441

Turkey Creek - Wyndham/Crocodile Farm | 100 | 4541

Wyndham - King River Restplace | 63 | 4604 | X

17 | King River Restplace - Kununurra | 116 | 4720

18 | Kununurra

19 | Kununurra

20 | Kununurra

21 | Kununurra

22 | Kununurra - Lake Argyle Tourist Village | 114 | 4834

23 | Lake Argyle Tourist Village - NT Border | 48 | 4882 | X

24 | NT Border - "62 Mile Restplace"/Victoria River | 413 | 5295

"62 Mile Restplace"/Victoria River - Katherine | 110 | 5405 | X

25 | Katherine - Nitmiluk NP/Katherine Gorge | 100 | 5505 | X

26 | Katherine - Edith Falls/Nitmiluk NPark | 60 | 5565

Edith Falls - Douglas Hot Springs NP | 192 | 5757

27 | Douglas Hot Springs NP - Bachelor | 130 | 5887

Bachelor - Litchfield National Park | 49 | 5936

28 | Litchfield National Park - Darwin | 362 | 6298 | X

Darwin - Darwin | 161 | 6459 | X

29 | Darwin - Jabiru/Kakadu NP | 369 | 6828

30 | Jabiru/Kakadu NP - Nourlangie Walk | 70 | 6898 | X

Nourlangie - Yellow Waters | 39 | 6937

31 | Yellow Waters - Katherine | 261 | 7198

Katherine - Mataranka /Elsey NP | 120 | 7318 | X

32 | Mataranka/Elsey National Park - Elliot | 329 | 7647

Elliot - Marry Ann /Tennant Creek | 255 | 7902 | X

33 | Marry Ann /Wauchope - Alice Springs/Wintersun | 533 | 8435 | X

34 | Alice Springs - Alice Springs | 30 | 8465 | Xx

35 | Alice Springs - Ormiston Gorge | 173 | 8638

36 | Ormiston Gorge - Mt. Sonder | 57 | 8695
37 | Glen Helen - Alice Springs | 159 | 8854
38 | Alice Springs - Erldunda | 112 | 8966 | X
39 | Erldunda - Curtin Springs | 148 | 9114
Curtin Springs - Yulara | 176 | 9290 | X
40| "Restplace" Yulara - Uluru/Ayers Rock | 30 | 9320
Uluru/Ayers Rock - Kata Tjuta/Olgas | 55 | 9375
Kata Tjuta/Olgas - Uluru/Ayers Rock | 55 | 9430
Uluru/Yulara - Curtin Springs | 89 | 9519 | X
41 | Curtin Springs - Kings Canyon | 228 | 9747
Kings Canyon - Mt. Ebenezer Roadhouse | 113 | 9860
42 | Mt. Ebenezer Roadhouse - Kulgera | 13 | 9873 | X
Kulgera - Marla | 183 | 10056
Marla - Cadney Roadhouse | 80 | 10136 | X
43 | Cadney Roadhouse - Breakaways | 160 | 10296
Breakaways - Coober Pedy | 30 | 10326
44 | Coober Pedy - Coober Pedy | 20 | 10346 | X
45 | Coober Pedy - Bon Bon Rest Area | 191 | 10537
46 | Bon Bon Rest Area - Woomera | 121 | 10658
Pimba - Hawker | 283 | 10941 | X
47 | Hawker - Flinders Ranges NP/Wilpena Pound | 137 | 11078
48 | Flinders Ranges NP/St Mary Peak
49 | Wilpena Pound - Quorn | 125 | 11203
50 | Quorn - Port Augusta | 156 | 11359 | X
51 | Port Augusta - Adelaide | 253 | 11612 | X
52 | Adelaide - Adelaide | 10 | 11622
53 | Adelaide - Murray Bridge | 80 | 11702
Murray Bridge - Naracoorte | 305 | 12007 | X
54 | Naracoorte

Endnotes and Links

1 The Pinnacles, WA http://goo.gl/maps/2qx6

2 A stretch of road with a Floodway sign, WA http://goo.gl/maps/7UMc2

3 Exmouth and North West Cape, WA https://goo.gl/maps/nVZHqMEyEjs

4 Yardie Creek, Cape Range National Park, WA https://goo.gl/maps/L9CdwFA-1JW62

5 Giant cracks of Karijini, WA https://goo.gl/maps/GP83yNJU1GA2

6 Banjima Drive, dirt road to gorges, WA https://goo.gl/maps/QzcKgnwojiR2

7 Railway crossing on Karijini Drive http://goo.gl/maps/djly

8 Karijini Gorges https://goo.gl/maps/C63pJ22QPVm

9 Mount Bruce, Western Australia https://goo.gl/maps/FRifcB8hcPA2

10 Sandfire Roadhouse on Great Northern Highway, WA http://goo.gl/maps/AE7A

11 Jas. S. Battye, The History of the North West of Australia. Perth, 1915, p. 8.

12 William Dampier, Dampier's Voyages, E. Grant Richardson, London, vol. 1, 1906, pp. 453-54

13 Japanese Cemetery in Broome http://goo.gl/maps/8JAl

14 China Wall near Halls Creek http://goo.gl/maps/Ba7V

15 Big crocodile in Wyndham https://goo.gl/maps/6kdWFB9LLP82

16 Big Aboriginal family in Wyndham http://goo.gl/maps/ShMZ

17 Giant crop fields of Kununurra, WA http://goo.gl/maps/0RLT

18 Lake Argyle, WA dam https://goo.gl/maps/J494ziv35bJ2

19 Argyle Diamond Mine https://goo.gl/maps/fQMpiNEjdcn

20 Cascading waterfalls Edith Falls, NT https://goo.gl/maps/43KBR8CZjJF2

21 Tjuwaliyn (Douglas) Hot Springs, NT https://goo.gl/maps/XEpxD3gy12J2

22 Havlik Park with Karlstein castle https://goo.gl/maps/9Nr6Nt5gZAA2

23 Darwin, NT https://goo.gl/maps/wKp3S7F9nHw

24 Nourlangie art site, NT https://goo.gl/maps/vcEiL91y1YF2

25 Mataranka and Elsey National Park https://goo.gl/maps/rVE4NQcgC1m

26 Daly Waters, NT https://goo.gl/maps/qqYWxYBzkkT2

27 Elliot, NT https://goo.gl/maps/ex82H4rAz6u

28 Karlu Karlu / Devils Marbles, NT https://goo.gl/maps/8d9GMmiCrLS2

29 Simpsons Gap, West McDonnell Ranges https://goo.gl/maps/dbSosh9iYbr

30 Ormiston Gorge, Northern Territory https://goo.gl/maps/pGb4jWPY9QB2

31 Old Ghan Museum near Alice Springs, NT https://goo.gl/maps/rpXEh-MagDfF2

32 What it's like to be a cyclist on Stuart Highway, NT https://goo.gl/maps/rpX-EhMagDfF2

33 Atilla/Mount Conner, NT https://goo.gl/maps/6E5sQ8azKyq

34 On the way to the Red Centre, NT https://goo.gl/maps/uoWHtkQDjNx

35 Uluru Sunset Viewing Area, NT https://goo.gl/maps/vSjkTxsBGdy

36 Kata Tjuta Valley of the Winds, NT https://goo.gl/maps/tteab6tLD8r

37 Strange landscape of Breakaways https://goo.gl/maps/bS4etxuyWCL2

38 Truck as a symbolic entrance to Coober Pedy https://goo.gl/maps/yRePYG5MbBL2

39 Warning sign before Coober Pedy https://goo.gl/maps/M2uzbhWsT4F2

40 Spaceship left behind by film-makers in Coober Pedy, SA https://goo.gl/maps/C2ujytDvn182

41 Dugout churches in Coober Pedy, SA https://goo.gl/maps/K4vA64kepsG2

42 It is easy to get lost outside the town of Coober Pedy, SA https://goo.gl/maps/EUPtbdmzke22

43 Sifting machinery in Coober Pedy, SA https://goo.gl/maps/LTTGfnPrmru

44 Rocket park in Woomera https://goo.gl/maps/uGkX9ZbEsUy

45 Road to Port Augusta with Flinders Ranges in the background, SA https://goo.

gl/maps/sY7NXvA3nBC2

46 Lake Hart, SA: beginning of a huge drainage basin https://goo.gl/maps/ue15NfBwrww

47 Wilpena Pound, SA that looks like meteor crater https://goo.gl/maps/vnytV7Zj9r42

48 St Mary Peak in Flinders Ranges https://goo.gl/maps/Ftrt2XSw3bF2

49 Big rocking horse in Gumeracha https://goo.gl/maps/6ftT7vBYk1q

50 Naracoorte Caves National Park https://goo.gl/maps/eBDG7f6KqNM2

51 Cliffs of the Grampians https://goo.gl/maps/5ChNpz1KyYo

52 Giant Koala https://goo.gl/maps/EbV7HHc2wUP2

53 Mount Zero Picnic Area https://goo.gl/maps/CVroDzRQxKr

54 London Bridge at Great Ocean Road, Victoria https://goo.gl/maps/YCmntpmE2os

55 Rough Victorian coast https://goo.gl/maps/YKMXwYeQ8Bt

56 A Victorian icon: Twelve Apostles https://goo.gl/maps/TYF2D7oFTex

57 William Ricketts Sanctuary, Victoria https://goo.gl/maps/Lqbot3kHsUA2

58 Strzelecki Memorial in Jindabyne, NSW https://goo.gl/maps/H4hEpByDZVn

59 Mount Kosciuszko, NSW https://goo.gl/maps/7MiPSN4XEFA2

60 Glow worm tunnel near Newnes, NSW https://goo.gl/maps/MVtoXzPdrJS2

61 Turon River, NSW https://goo.gl/maps/ML9MnvoMK6n

62 Holtermann Collection at State Library, NSW: http://www2.sl.nsw.gov.au/archive/discover_collections/society_art/photography/holtermann/

63 History Hill, Hill End, NSW https://goo.gl/maps/J8Q23rEUhFU2

55 | Naracoorte - Mt Arapiles | 199 12206 | X
56 | Mt Arapiles - Stawell | 170 | 12376
57 | Stawell - Grampians NP/Wonderland | 90 | 12466
58 | Stawell - Grampians NP/Mt Stapylton | 116 | 12582 | X
59 | Stawell - Warrnambool | 308 | 12890
60 | Warrnambool | X
61 | Warrnambool - Lorne/Cumberland Carpark | 271 | 13161
62 | Lorne - Torquay | 76 | 13237
63 | Torquay - Melbourne | 120 | 13357 | X
64 | Melbourne
65 | Melbourne
66 | Melbourne
67 | Melbourne - Melbourne | 349 | 13706
68 | Melbourne - Benalla | 248 | 13954 | X
69 | Benalla - Bright/Mt Buffalo NP | 106 | 14060
70 | Bright - Corryong | 206 | 14266
71 | Corryong - Jindabyne | 120 | 14386 | X
72 | Jindabyne - Kosciuszko NP/Ngarigo | 36 | 14422
Kosciuszko NP/Dead Horse Gap - Jindabyne | 100 | 14522
73 | Jindabyne/Caravan Park - Canberra | 218 | 14740
74 | Canberra - Canberra | 50 | 14790 | X
75 | Canberra - Goulburn/Kialla | 192 | 14982 | X
76 | Kialla - Oberon | 159 | 15141
77 | Oberon - Jenolan Caves | 74 | 15215
78 | Jenolan Caves - Leura/Blue Mountains NP | 81 | 15296 | X
79 | Leura - Lithgow | 165 | 15461
80 | Lithgow - Newnes/Wollemi NP | 48 | 15509
81 | Newnes - Bathurst | 84 | 15593
82 | Bathurst - Hill End | 75 | 15668

83 | Hill End - Hill End | 117 | 15785 | X
84 | Hill End - Bathurst | 75 | 15860
Bathurst - Sydney | 201 | 16061 | X

Travel Budget Hints

ITEM: % of budget

Petrol: 23.3 % (A); refuelling 46 times

Food: 23.4 % (B);

Equipment: 11.1 % (C)

Car maintenance, registration, penalties, fines: 15.4 % (D)

Accommodation: 10.8 % (E)

National park fees: 2.75 % (F)

Miscellaneous: 13.25 % (G)

Based on this information you can easily calculate the very minimum cost of a budget travel through the continent, e. g.:

Assuming consumption of 9 litres of petrol per 100 km: 46 refuellings *times* the size of your petrol/diesel tank *times* current price of 1 litre petrol/diesel = A

At the time of our journey an average bread roll cost twice the price of one litre of petrol. If price of petrol or diesel shoots up, the food share on the total budget will have to be adjusted accordingly. This way you can calculate "B".

We don't live of bread only but this will do as a very rough estimate. The ratio of the two items tells a lot about the current price level and works surprisingly well.

C, D, E, F, and G can then be calculated from the percentages.

Not to forget

A first-aid kit in a car is not compulsory in Australia, but it should be the first thing any sensible and serious traveller buys. They often sell them with survival and emergency handbooks. Carry both of those items with you all the time

A good torch can be handy in many situations. Carry most of the times

2 sets of thongs: showers in the outback are often dirty

Personal hygiene

Basic medicine

Suncream: lots and lots of it

Sun glasses: buy more and have them always within arm's reach

Water container: it needs to be kept full all the time

Fuel container: it might not be necessary but it can be helpful

Pencil tyre gauge

Dust pan and brush

Battery charger, jump start kit

Spray cleaner

Kitchen utensils, travel dishes, fry pan

Good sleeping bags and pillows

Good mattresses

Tent

Gas burner and fuel cartridges

Good knife with can opener; basic tool box

Maps and guides

Esky with ice packs

Fly net

Insect repellent

"Tyreseal"/tyre-fixing kit

Plastic box that can be used as both storage and table

Wrench, hammer, small axe

Hot water bottle / container

Metal kettle that can be put on fire or burner

Water-resistant clothing and shoes. As for the shoes: good sturdy trekking shoes might be too warm in the north but will become a life-saver in the south, especially when hiking in the mountains

Candles lighter, matches

Needle and thread/sewing kit
Large plastic bags
Air pump
Useful shops/sites:
    Car part supplies: Repco, AutoOne, Supercheapauto
    DIY/camping supplies: Bunnings, Mitre 10, Masters
    Electrical: Jaycar Electronics
    Mattresses: Clarke Rubber
    Large foodstore/grocery chains: Aldi (best value for money), Woolworths, Coles, Iga
    Non-grocery/camping: K-Mart, Target, Big W
    Miscellaneous/Discount: any "one dollar shop" in large shopping centres like Dollar King, Reject Shop etc.
    Second-hand items: Vinnies (St Vincent de Paul Society), Salvos (Salvation Army), Anglicare (Anglican Church)
    Cars: carsales.com.au, ozcar.com.au

Bibliography

Bailey, John. White Divers of Broome (The true story of a fatal experiment). Sydney: Pan Macmillan Australia Pty Ltd, 2002.

Jas. S. Battye. The History of the North West of Australia. Perth, 1915

Haill, Robert G. Opals of the Never Never. Cammeray: Horwitz Grahame Books Pty Ltd, 1981.

Elwood, Paul. Around Australia by Bicycle: The Complete Guide. Elwood, Paul, 2003.

Drinkwater, M. The German-Australian called Holtermann (Ein Deutsch-Australier namens Holtermann. Sydney: Malcolm Drinkwater, 1985.

Baker, Robert G.V. The Second Rush (A Study of the Second Goldrush to Sofala in 1851. Cronulla: Centre Pak Research, 1986.

Thomas Tyrone T. 50 Walks in the Grampians. Melbourne: Hill of Content, 1983.

Department of Environment and Conservation. Karijini National Park Information and Walk Trail.

Pilger, John. A Secret Country, London: Vintage, 1992.

Mundle, Rob. Flinders: The Man who Mapped Australia. Sydney: Hachette Australia Pty Limited, 2012.

Spencer, Sir Walter Baldwin. The Native Tribes of Central Australia: Adamant Media Corporation, 2000.

Phelps, James. Australia's Most Murderous Prison: Behind the Walls of Goulburn Jail. North Sydney: Random House Australia Pty. Ltd., 2015.

Korzeliński, Seweryn. Opis podróży do Australii i pobytu tamże od r. 1852 do 1856: Państwowy Instytut Wydawniczy, 1954

Korzelinski, Seweryn; Robe, Stanley. Memoirs of Gold-Digging in Australia

Index

A

Aboriginal paintings 124
Aboriginal rebels. *See* Jandamarra
Adelaide 177
Adelaide River 117
Adnyamathanha. *See* Wilpena Pound
Afghans 138
air con. *See* air conditioning
air conditioning 45
Alice Springs 134
Alice Springs Telegraph Station 134
ANZAC 113
ANZAC Day 112
Anzac Hill, Alice Springs 134
April 25 112
Arrernte people 135
Atilla. *See* Mount Conner
Atilla, Mount Conner 143
ATMs 48
Ayers Rock. *See* Uluru
Azaria, Chamberlain 152

B

back-burning 119
Bana, Eric 201
Banjima Drive 62
Barramundi Gap 110
Barrow Creek 133
bats, Mataranka 128
Baudin, Commodore Nicholas 78
bends. *See* decompression disease
Beyers, Hugo Luis 223
bicentenary 30
Big Aboriginal family, Wyndham 98
Big crocodile. Wyndham 97
Big Koala. *See* Giant Koala
Big Rocking Horse, Gumeracha 177
billabong 125
bindies 47

Binnu 52
Bird Rock, Grampians 184
bob trailer 75
Bowali Visitor Centre 122
Breakaways 154
Brett, David 153
Bridle Track 217
Broome 76, 78, 78–85
Broome, Sir Frederick Napier 82
Bufo Marinus. *See* cane toad
Buley Rock Hole 118
Bungle Bungle National Park 95
bush shower 71

C

cam belt 45
Canberra 211
cane toad 76
Cape of Good Hope 192
Cape Range National Park 59
Carnarvon 56
Cathedral Termite Mound 118
cattle grid 51, 55
Centennial Park 199
Centipede 164
Chamberlain 152
Charles Hotham 194
Charles Joseph La Trobe 194
Charlie 209
China Wall 96
Chopper 197, 197–203
cockatoo 69, 194
Colac Colac 205
common sense 64
Coober Pedy 156–170
Cooinda 125
Cook, James 31
Coral Bay 57
corn detasseling 101, 104
corrugated road 62
Crimean War 194
crocodile 99, 116, 122

crocodile farm, Kakadu 122
crocodile farm, Wyndham 98
Crossing Inn, pub 90
Cumberland River Holiday Park 189
currawong bird 176
Curtin Springs 143
cyclone Tracy 119

D

Dalesford, Victoria 192
Daly Waters 131
damper 170
Dampier, WA 70
Dampier, William 79
Dandenong Ranges 203
Darwin 87, 119–120
Darwin nude beach 119
David Brett 153
Dead Horse Gap 206
decompression disease 81
Devils Marbles 133, 134
diamond mine 110
dingo 73, 123
Dingo case 152–153
Diprotodon optatum 178
Dirt Holes Creek 220
Dodger. *See* Roger Dodger Rogerson
Douglas Hot Springs 117
duty of care 67

E

Edith Falls 115, 116
Elliot 132
El Questro 99
Elwood, Paul 75
Emma Gorge 99
emu 39, 59
Emu 170
Erldunda Caravan Park 139
Esplanade Hotel, Framantle 42
Eureka Stockade 196
Exmouth Gulf 58

F

Falconio, Peter 133
Fisher, Malcolm Dr. 53
Fitzroy Crossing 94
flies 134
Flinders, Matthew 174
Flinders Ranges. *See* Ikara-Flinders Ranges
Floriade 211
flying fox 128
Ford Falcon 37, 38, 88
Free Coffee for Driver 52, 132
Fremantle 40
Freo. *See* Fremantle
freshie, fresh water crocodile 107
fruit bat. *See* flying fox

G

Gallipoli 112
Gariwerd. *See* Grampians
Geiki Gorge 94
Geiki, Sir Archibald 94
Geraldton 51, 52
Ghan Museum 138
giant kangaroo. *See* Procoptodon goliah
Giant Koala near Stawell 183
giant wombat 178. *See* Diprotodon optatum
Gibb River Road 99
Gillen, Francis James 135
Glow Worm Tunnel 216
Go, game 154
Golden Orb Spider 47
goon 78
Grampians 181–187
Grand Canyon, Grampians 182
Great Barrier Reef 58
Great Depression 158
Great Ocean Road 188
Great Sandy Desert 76
Gulgong, Holtermann Museum 225
Gumeracha 177

H

half cast 80
Halls Creek 96
Hamersley, Edward 68
Hamersley Ranges 68
Hancock Gorge 68
Hancock, Lang 61
Handrail Pool, Karijini 69
Hargraves, Edward Hammond 220
Havlik Park 117
Hayes Creek 117
Hidden Valley Caravan Park 120
Hill End 216, 217–226
History Hill 226
Holden 38
Hollow Mountain, Grampians 182, 187
Holtermann, Otto Bernard 223
Hotham, Charles 194
Huckstepp, Sallie-Anne 199
huntsman, spider 53
Hutchinson, Bill 158

I

Ikara. *See* Ikara-Flinders Ranges
Ikara-Flinders Ranges 172–176
indigenous 24, 30, 79, 162
inselberg 143
invasion 30
iron ore 68

J

Jabiru 122, 124
Jackie 209
Jandamarra 88
Japanese Cemetery in Broome 85
Jenolan Caves 214
Jim Crow 192
Jindabyne 206
Joffre Falls 70
Joffre Gorge 68
Johns, Ronnie 201
junkyards 46, 123
Jurien Bay 50, 51

K

Kaiser Steel 61
Kakadu National Park 120, 121–125
kamikaze 86
Kanangra Boyd 214
kangaroos 46, 58, 60–244
karaoke 115
Karijini 61
Karijini Drive 68, 74
Karijini gorges
  Hancock Gorge 68
  Joffre Gorge 68
  Knox Gorge 68
  Red Gorge 68
  Weano Gorge 68
  Wittenoom Gorge 68
Karijini National Park 68
Karlstein, castle 117
Karlu Karlu. *See* Devils Marbles
Karlu Karlu, Devil's Marbles 134
Kata Tjuta (The Olgas, Mount Olga) 142, 144, 149
Katherine Gorge 114
Kelly, Ned 197
Kimberley Range 81
Kings Canyon 149
Knox Gorge 68
kookaburra 41
Korzelinski, Seweryn 190
Kremlin 129
Kulgera 154
Kununurra 101–104

L

Lake Argyle 106–109, 111
Lake Eyre 173
Lake Hart 173
Lanfranchi, Warren 199
Larapinta Trail 134, 138
La Trobe 194
Lees, Joanne 133
Lenin's tomb 129
Lenin, Vladimir Ilyich 129

Lennon, John 130
Leopold Downs Road 87
Lindy Chamberlain 152
Lister, John 220
Litchfield National Park 118
London Bridge 188

M

Mabo case 34
Mabo, Eddie Koiki 31, 32
Mad Max 154
Malabanjbandju Caravan Area 122, 124
Mango Camping Area 83
Maralinga 170
Mataranka 127
Matsu Range 110
McArthur, James 209
Melbourne 190, 192
Melbourne Cup 84
Mendeleev, Dmitri 219
Milat, Ivan 92–93
Mindil Beach Sunset Market 119
missionaries 34
Monaghan's Bluff 217
monsoon rain 55
Moscow 129
mosquitoes 122, 124
mother-of-pearl 78
Mount Bruce, Punurrunha 70, 71, 73
Mount Buffalo 205
Mount Conner 143
Mount Frederick 73
Mount King 73
Mount Kosciuszko 206–211
Mount Meharry 73
Mount Nameless 73
Mount Olga 149
Mount Sonder 136, 137
Mount Stapylton 184
Mount Townsend 208
Mount Vigors 73
Müller, Sir Ferdinand Jacob Heinrich von 148

Murdoch, Bradley John 133
Murray Island, Queensland 32

N

Nambung National Park 50
nanny state 64
Naracoorte 178
NASA 106, 147
Native Title to Land 34
Nerve Test 181
New Holland 31, 209
Newnes 215
New South Wales 205
Ngariro Campground 207
Ngarri Mudlanha. *See* St Mary Peak
Ningaloo Marine Park 58
Nitmiluk National Park 115
noodling 134
noodling machinery 167
North West Cape Peninsula 58
Nourlangie Rock Art Site 124

O

Ochre Pits 136
octopus as God 34
OH&S 108
Oil shell refinery 215
oil-shell rock 215
Old Ghan 139
Olgas. *See* Kata Tjuta (The Olgas, Mount Olga)
Onions, Paul 92–93
opal 134, 157
Ophir 220
Orange 220
Ormiston Campground 136
Ormiston Gorge 136
ostrich 39

P

Paraburdoo 60, 68
Pavlova, ballerina 43
Pavlova, cake 44

permanent residency 90
Perth 41
Petersham 199
petrol stations 46
Phillip, Arthur 30
Pichi Richi 175
Pierce, Alexander 197
Pinnacles 50, 52
Port Augusta 172, 173
Port Hedland 74, 76
possum 41, 194
potch 159, 167
Pound Walk 136
Price, Thomas Moore 61
Procoptodon goliah 178
Pteropus. *See* flying fox
Punurrunha 72
Purnululu. *See* Bungle Bungle National Park

R

Read, Mark Brandon Chopper 197
redback. spider 40
Redbank Gorge 137
Red Centre 138, 142–149
Red Gorge 68
Reservoir Dogs 201
rest places 47
Ricketts, William 203
Riley, James 209
Rocket park, Woomera 171
"Rocky Open Legs" 149
Roger Dodger Rogerson 198
Rwetyepme. *See* Mount Sonder

S

saltie, salt water crocodile 107
Sandfire Roadhouse 76
Sandy Billabong, tragedy 125
Savannah campground, Karijini 70
Seweryn Korzelinski 190
Sex on the Beach 164
Sexy Walls 149

Shady Glen Caravan Park 119
sheep 51
Shithouse, Daly Waters 131
Shore, Anglican private school 224
shovel-nosed catfish. *See* silver cobbler
siege of Sevastopol 194
Silent Street, Grampians 182
silver cobbler, fish 110
Simpsons Gap 135
Sir Charles Hotham 196
Snowy Mountains 206
Sofala 217
Sow and Piglets 189
spear-thrower, Woomera 170
Spencer, Sir Walter Baldwin 135
spiders
  Golden Orb Spider 47
  huntsman 53
  redback 40
spinifex 82
Squashed Frog 164
"squirrelcats" 41
S.S. Great Britain 190
Star of Hope 223
St Basil's Cathedral 129
St Mary Peak 175
stolen generation 81
Strzelecki, Sir Paul Edmund 209
Stuart Highway 116
Stuart, John McDuall 116
Sydney, First Viscount 208
Sydney Harbour Bridge 225

T

Tambaroora 220
Tarunda Caravan Park 89
Telstra 47
Tennant Creek 132
terra nullius 32
thongs 48
Three Ways 132
timing belt. *See* cam belt

Tjuwaliyn. *See* Douglas Hot Springs
Todd River 134
Tom, James 220
Tom Price 60, 61
Torquay 189

Townsend, Thomas 208

Toyota Corolla 38
trekking bike 140
tucker 79
Tunnel Creek 87
Turkey Creek 95
Turon River 220
Twelve Apostles 189

U

Uluru 133, 141, 142, 144, 148

V

Valley of the Winds 149
Vlaming Head 59

W

Wakayama province 84
Walpa Gorge Walk 149
Warmun Roadhouse 95
Warrnambool 188
Weano Gorge 68
West MacDonnell Ranges 135–138
Wheatley, Gordon 53
White Australia policy 83
Wilpena Pound 175
Windjana Gorge 87
Wintersun Caravan Park 134
Wittenoom Gorge 68
Wolfe Creek Crater 96
Wollemia nobilis. *See* Wollemi Pine
Wollemi National Park 214
Woomera 170
work and holiday visa 55
Work and Holiday visa 90
Wyndham 97

Y

YAK-52 130
Yardie Creek 59
Yorkies Creek 220
Yulara 145, 149

Z

zebra rock 110

www.ingramcontent.com/pod-product-compliance
Lightning Source LLC
Chambersburg PA
CBHW032151080426
42735CB00008B/671